POSTCARDS 3

Brian Abbs
Chris Barker
Ingrid Freebairn
with **Stella Reilly**

LONGMAN ON THE **WEB**

Longman.com offers online resources for teachers and students. Access our Companion Websites, our online catalog, and our local offices around the world.

Visit us at **longman.com**.

Longman

Postcards 3

Pearson Education, 10 Bank Street, White Plains, NY 10606

Editorial director: Ed Lamprich
Senior development editor: Marilyn Hochman
Development editor: Julie Schmidt
Vice president, director of design and production: Rhea Banker
Executive managing editor: Linda Moser
Production manager: Liza Pleva
Associate managing editor: Mike Kemper
Director of manufacturing: Patrice Fraccio
Senior manufacturing buyer: Nancy Flaggman
Photo research: Aerin Csigay
Cover design: Ann France
Text design: Ann France and Pearson Education
  Development Group
Text font: 11/14 palatino
Text composition: Pearson Education Development Group

ISBN: 0-13-092591-8

4 5 6 7 8 9 10–WC–08 07 06 05

Acknowledgments

Pearson Education would like to thank the following teachers for their invaluable suggestions during the development of *Postcards 3*:

Reviewers

Angelita Moreno, Brazil • **Vagner Luis Mastropoulo**, Brazil • **Roberto Lobo**, Brazil • **Patricia Iglesias Goncalves**, Brazil • **Marcela Quesada Alvarado**, Costa Rica • **Marc Chevalier**, Chile • **Claudia Amaya**, Colombia • **Juan Omar Valdez**, Dominican Republic • **María Cristina Merodio Tamés**, Mexico • **Blanca Jiménez León**, Mexico • **Noela Cartaya de Herrero**, Venezuela • **Abigail Polivoda**, Venezuela

Contributors

Charles Green for writing the activities for the songs, the games, the projects, the Wide Angle readings, and the Zoom in on culture readings. • **David McKeegan** for writing the "Let's Get Started" unit.

Illustration credits

pp. 3, 59 Jim Starr; pp. 10, 12, 19, 25, 32, 35, 56, 63, 84, 91, 92, 98, 100 Mike Hortens; pp. 20, 36, 82 Anna Veltfort; pp. 21, 26 Tim Haggerty; p. 30 Ellen Beier; pp. 38, 39 Roxanna Baer-Block; p. 42 Ron Young; pp. 66-67 Robert Roper; pp. 70, 87 Ron Zalme; p. 76 Chris Reed; p. 78 Brian Hughes; p. 86 Frank Sofo; p. 101 Hal Just; p. 34 Peter Gunther

Text credits

p.8 Courtesy of CBS News, A Division of CBS Broadcasting Inc. Copyright © 2001 CBS Worldwide Inc. All Rights Reserved; p.22 Jenny Carstairs; p.30 "I Need To Know." Words and Music by Cory Rooney and Marc Anthony. Copyright © 1999 Song/ATV Songs LLC, Cori Tiffani Publishing and Sony/ATV Tunes LLC. This arrangement Copyright © 2003 Sony/ATV Songs LLC, Cori Tiffani Publishing and Sony/ATV Tunes LLC. All Rights Administered by Sony/ATV Music Publishing, 8 Music Square West, Nashville, TN 37203. International Copyright Secured. All Rights Reserved; p.56 www.parentteen.com; p. 58 "Hanging By A Moment." Words and Music by Jason Wade. Copyright © 2000 Songs of DreamWorks (BMI) and G Chills Music (BMI). This arrangement Copyright © 2002 Songs of DreamWorks (BMI) and G Chills Music (BMI). Worldwide Rights for Songs of DreamWorks and G Chills Music Administered by Cherry River Music Co. International Copyright Secured. All Rights Reserved; p.86 "Crash And Burn." Words and Music by Darren Hayes and Daniel Jones. © 1999 Rough Cut Music & WB Music Corp. (ASCAP). All Rights for Rough Cut Music Administered by WB Music Corp. Lyrics Reprint by Permission of Warner Bros. Publications, Miami, FL 33014. All Rights Reserved.

Photo credits

All original photography by Michal Heron; p.2 (left) RubberBall Productions/Getty Images, (right) PhotoDisc/Getty Images; p.6 (1) Popperfoto, (2) Popperfoto, (3) Scope Features, (4) Sygma, (5) All-Action; p.8 Courtesy of CBS News, A Division of CBS Broadcasting Inc. Copyright © 2001 CBS Worldwide Inc. All Rights Reserved; p.10 (top) Don Tremain; p.14 (top left) D. Boone/Corbis, (top right) Laurence Fordyce/Eye Ubiquitous/Corbis, (bottom left) Sandy Felsenthal/Corbis, (bottom right) John Neubauer/PhotoEdit; p.16 (top) Digital Vision/Getty Images, (bottom) PhotoDisc/Getty Images; p.17 Penny Tweedie/Getty Images; p.22 AWL/by Peter Lake; p.24 Duomo/Corbis; p.28 (top) Reuters NewMedia Inc./Corbis, (bottom) David Strick/Corbis Outline; p.30 Reuters NewMedia Inc./Corbis; p.31 (top left) Frank Micelotta/Getty Images, (top right) AFP/Corbis, (middle left) The Kobal Collection/The Picture Desk, (middle) David Cannon/Laureus/Getty Images, (middle right) AFP/Corbis, (bottom left) Jonathan Player/Camera Press/Retna, Ltd., (bottom right) Duomo/Corbis; p.44 Paramount/The Kobal Collection/The Picture Desk; p.45 (top) NASA/Johnson Space Center, (bottom) Corbis KIPA; p.48 RubberBall Productions/PictureQuest; p.49 Carlos Alvarez/Getty Images; p.50 (left) Alan Becker/Getty Images, (right) Stockbyte/PictureQuest; p.55 Barbara Penoyar/Getty Images; p.56 (left) SW Productions/Getty Images, (middle) David Young-Wolff/PhotoEdit, (right) Kevin Peterson/Getty Images; p.58 (top) S. Reincke/Retna, Ltd., (left) Ryan McVay/Getty Images, (right) SW Productions/Getty Images; p.62 Courtesy of Six Flags Theme Parks; p.63 Courtesy of Six Flags Theme Parks; p.64 Courtesy of Six Flags Theme Parks; p.65 Donna Day/Getty Images; p.72 (top) Photofest, (bottom) Photofest; p.73 Warner Bros TV/Bright/Kauffman/Crane Productions/The Kobal Collection/The Picture Desk; p.75 Kevin Fleming/Corbis; p.77 (1) Joseph Sohm; ChromoSohm Inc./Corbis, (2) Peter Johnson/Corbis, (3) AP/Wide World Photos, (4) Globe Photos, (5) AP/Wide World Photos, (6) AP/Wide World Photos, (7) AP/Wide World Photos, (8) Photofest, (9) Globe Photos; p.78 Dreamworks/Universal /Buitendijk, JAAP/The Kobal Collection/The Picture Desk; p.86 Spiros Politis/Retna, Ltd.; p.93 (full page) Cameron Davidson/Folio, Inc., (top right) Bequest of Mrs. Benjamin Ogle Tayloe; Collection of the Corcoran Gallery of Art/Corbis, (right) Todd Gipstein/ Corbis, (middle) Peter Gridley/Getty Images, (bottom left) Richard T. Nowitz/Corbis; p.94 (top) David A. Northcott/Corbis, (middle) AFP/Corbis, (bottom) Kelley-Mooney Photography/ Corbis; p.95 (top left and right) Rex Features, (middle left) Alpha/Globe Photos, (middle right) Tristar/Amblin/Ricco Torres/The Kobal Collection/The Picture Desk, (right) Star Max, Inc./Corbis KIPA, (bottom left) Despotovic Dusko/Corbis Sygma; p.96 (top) Dorling Kindersley Media Library, (bottom) Will & Deni McIntyre/Getty Images; p.97 (top) Robert Frerck/ Odyssey Productions, Inc., (bottom) Reuters NewMedia Inc./ Corbis; p.98 (top) PhotoDisc/Getty Images, (middle left) Corbis, (middle right) Michael S. Yamashita/Corbis, (bottom) Michael S. Yamashita/Corbis; p.99 (top) Bo Zaunders/Corbis, (middle) Bob Krist/Corbis, (right) Roberto Soncin Gerometta/Photo 20-20/ PictureQuest; pp.100-101 (full page) David Ball/Corbis, p.100 (top) Kevin R. Morris/Corbis, (bottom left) Bohemian Nomad Picturemakers/Corbis, (bottom right) Carl & Ann Purcell/Corbis; p.101 (top) Neil Setchfield/The Travelsite/The Picture Desk, (bottom) AP/Wide World Photos.

Cover photos: White water rafting: Corbis Stock Market; Roller Coaster: Kwame Zikomo/SuperStock, Inc.; Riverwalk, San Antonio, Texas: Sandy Felsenthal/Corbis; Cowboy Boots with Spurs: Getty Images, Inc.

Contents

Scope and Sequence

Unit	Title	Communication	Grammar
1 Pages 4–9	**We usually meet at 4:00.**	• Introduce oneself to a group	• Simple present contrasted with the present continuous • Position of adverbs of frequency
2 Pages 10–14	**It was quite an experience!**	• Make suggestions • Express preferences	• Simple past tense: regular and irregular verbs
Page 15	**Progress Check**		
Pages 16–17	**Wide Angle 1:** Parents and Teens: Living with Each Other		
3 Pages 18–23	**Do I have to?**	• Talk about obligations	• *Have to:* simple present and simple past forms
4 Pages 24–28	**Who's going to the game?**	• Express future plans and activities	• The present continuous to express future time • Verb + infinitive
Page 29	**Progress Check**		
Page 30	**Song 1:** I Need to Know		
Page 31	**Game 1:** Mystery Celebrity		
5 Pages 32–37	**I'll have a sandwich.**	• Order food items and drinks	• *Will* and *won't* for decisions, promises, and future predictions • The imperative
6 Pages 38–42	**If you need me, I'll be there.**	• Describe personalities	• Adjectives and adverbs • *If* clauses to express future meaning
Page 43	**Progress Check**		
Pages 44–45	**Wide Angle 2:** The '70s		

Vocabulary	Skills	Learn to Learn	Pronunciation
Teen Activities	*Reading:* Scan an article for specific information; read for the main idea *Listening:* Listen for the main idea and specific details *Writing:* Write sentences using the present continuous and the simple present tense with adverbs of frequency *Speaking:* Introduce oneself to a group; talk about favorite activities		The sounds /st/, /sk/, and /sp/
Review of common adjectives: antonyms	*Reading:* Read for specific details *Listening:* Listen for information and specific details *Writing:* Write a dialogue in which speakers make suggestions, accept or reject suggestions, and express preference *Speaking:* Make suggestions; accept or reject suggestions; express preference		Dropped vowels in middle syllables
Household chores	*Reading:* Read for details *Listening:* Listen for details *Writing:* Write a paragraph about responsibilities at home *Speaking:* Talk about obligations		The reduced forms of *have to* and *has to*
Sports and sports locations	*Reading:* Scan a reading to find specific facts *Listening:* Listen for specific details to complete an itinerary *Writing:* Write interview questions for a celebrity based on a reading *Speaking:* Express future plans and activities; role-play an interview with a celebrity		
Food items and drinks Dance and exercise verbs	*Reading:* Read for details; read a map *Listening:* Listen to understand a sequence of steps *Writing:* Write directions to a place; write a sequence of dance steps *Speaking:* Give instructions, telling someone how to perform dance steps	Listening to native speakers of English to improve pronunciation	The sounds of /tʃ/ and /dʒ/
Adjectives with negative prefixes	*Reading:* Read and answer a questionnaire on personalities; read descriptions of personalities; understand meaning from context *Listening:* Listen for details *Writing:* Write sentences with adverbs of manner, write sentences with *if* clauses to express future meaning *Speaking:* Describe your own personality and the personality of others		Word stress in adjectives

Vocabulary	Skills	Learn to Learn	Pronunciation
Clothes and personal possessions	*Reading:* Read for (specific) information; read to make inferences *Listening:* Listen for details *Writing:* Write a paragraph about influences on teens when they buy clothes *Speaking:* Survey classmates about what influences them when they buy clothes		The sounds /b/ and /v/
Expressions related to school	*Reading:* Read for specific details *Listening:* Listen for specific details *Writing:* Write a paragraph expressing an opinion *Speaking:* Express opinions		
Adjectives of measurement	*Reading:* Read for details; read to make inferences *Listening:* Listen for specific details *Writing:* Write a paragraph describing the most exciting or the most unforgettable experience *Speaking:* Describe the most exciting or the most unforgettable experience	Reading maps in brochures and guides	
Action verbs	*Reading:* Read for (specific) information; read to make inferences *Listening:* Listen for specific details *Writing:* Create a poster of the different ways people can help others *Speaking:* Tell a story about someone who performs a small act of kindness		Words beginning with *r-* blends
Types of TV shows	*Reading:* Read for specific information and the main idea *Listening:* Listen for specific information; listen to make inferences *Writing:* Write sentences using the passive voice; write a dialogue asking for and giving additional information *Speaking:* Asking for and giving additional information	Learning English through movies and TV shows	
Extracurricular activities	*Reading:* Read for specific details; read to make inferences *Listening:* Listen for specific details; listen to make inferences *Writing:* Make a list of the benefits of extracurricular activities; use research and interview methods *Speaking:* Interview people to gather information	Developing your potential through after-school activities	

Stacy   Steve   Ms. Costa

Justin   Tom   Nicole

Let's get started.

1 Describing people

A. Form groups of three. Look at the pictures and the descriptions below. Quickly write ten sentences about Julia and Nathan in your notebook. Use the simple present form of *be* and *have* along with the pronouns *he, she,* and *they*. The first group to write ten correct sentences is the winner.

Examples:

1. *He is a tourist.*

2. *She is a doctor.*

3. *They are (both) happy.*

B. Work with a partner. In your notebook, write ten *Yes/No* questions about the pictures below. Then exchange questions with your partner and write short answers.

Examples:

1. *Is Nathan 40 years old?*

   Yes, he is.

2. *Do Nathan and Julia both have sunglasses?*

   No, they don't.

Name: Julia Rollins **Age:** 30

Name: Nathan Barley **Age:** 40

2 Twenty Questions

Work in groups of four or five. One student thinks of a place, for example, a city or a country. The other students try to find out what the place is by asking *Yes/No* questions. They can ask a maximum of twenty questions.

Example:

B: Is it in South America?
A: No, it isn't.
C: Is it cold there?
A: Yes, it is.

3 Puzzle

Write the past-tense form of the verbs below to complete the puzzle.

Across	Down
2 get	1 hug
4 sing	3 tell
6 say	5 sleep
7 drive	6 stand
8 buy	11 eat
9 go	
10 drink	
12 feel	

We usually meet at 4:00.

Learning Goals

Communication
Introduce oneself to a group

Grammar
Simple present contrasted with the present continuous
Position of adverbs of frequency

Vocabulary
Teen activities

1 Dialogue

🎧 **Listen and read.**

Ms. Costa: Welcome to the Foreign Language Club. I'm Ms. Costa. I'm the club adviser, OK? Now, can you tell me your name, your grade level, and the foreign language you're taking right now? OK?

Stacy: My name's Stacy. I'm in 11th grade, and I'm studying German.

Justin: I'm Justin, Justin Carlson. I'm in 12th grade, and I'm taking French.

Steve: My name's Stephen Liu. Steve for short. I'm taking Italian. I'm in 11th grade like Stacy.

Nicole: Hi! My name's Nicole Green. I'm learning Spanish. I'm a senior.

Tom: Thomas Bryant. You can call me Tom. I'm taking Spanish with Nicole. We're both in 12th grade. *(whispering)* Hey, Justin. What are you doing?

Justin: *(whispering)* I'm counting the number of times Ms. Costa says "OK." Listen.

Ms. Costa: OK. The club usually meets after school from 4 P.M. to 5 P.M. Tuesdays and Thursdays. But because it's the first day, we're finishing early. OK?

Justin: *(snickering)* See what I mean?

2 Comprehension

Read each sentence. Write the name of the person.

Ms. Costa   1. She's the club adviser.

_____ 2. He's studying Italian.

_____ 3. He's taking French.

_____ 4. She's studying German.

_____ 5. He's Nicole's classmate.

3 Pronunciation

The sounds /st/, /sk/, and /sp/

A. 🎧 Listen and repeat.

/st/	/sk/	/sp/
start	scary	Spanish
study	school	speak
Steve	skating	spot

B. 🎧 Listen to each word. Then write the first sound in the word, *st*, *sk*, or *sp* on the line.

1. _st_
2. ___
3. ___
4. ___

4 Useful Phrases

🎧 **Listen and repeat.**

- You can call me Tom.
- Steve for short.
- See what I mean?

5 Communication

Introducing yourself to a group

A. 🎧 Listen and repeat.

- I'm Thomas Bryant. You can call me Tom.
- My name's Stephen Liu. Steve for short.
- I'm in the 11th grade.

B. Form small groups and introduce yourself. Say your name and grade level.

The simple present contrasted with the present continuous

Simple present		
I	usually	**study** until 9:00.
He She }	usually	**studies** until 9:00.
You We They }	usually	**study** until 9:00.

Present continuous	
I	**'m studying** right now.
He She }	**'s studying** right now.
You We They }	**'re studying** right now.

Remember! Use the simple present tense to describe a habitual action. Use the present continuous to describe an activity that is happening right now.

6 Practice

In your notebook, write what each famous person in the picture is doing. Then write what the person usually does. Use the cues below.

1. A. Leonardo DiCaprio/sing
   B. He/act in movies

   Leonardo DiCaprio is singing.

   He usually acts in movies.

2. A. Elton John/play the guitar
   B. He/play the piano
3. A. Pavarotti/play soccer
   B. He/sing opera
4. A. Martina Hingis/sing
   B. She/play tennis
5. A. Tiger Woods/play tennis
   B. He/play golf

7 Your Turn

Work with a partner. Ask each other the questions below. Answer in complete sentences.

1. What magazines do you usually read?
2. What magazines are you reading right now?
3. What kinds of clothes do you usually wear?
4. What are you wearing right now?

1. Leonardo DiCaprio
2. Elton John
3. Pavarotti
4. Martina Hingis
5. Tiger Woods

GRAMMAR FOCUS

Position of adverbs of frequency

With be

Justin is { always / usually / often / sometimes / rarely / never } late.

With other verbs

Stacy { always / usually / often / sometimes / rarely / never } gets up late.

How often is Justin late? He is **never** late.
How often does Stacy get up late? She **always** gets up late.
How often can you stay out late? I can **never** stay out late.

Remember!

• Adverbs of frequency answer the question *How often?*
• Adverbs of frequency come **after** the verb *be*, but **before** other verbs.
• Some frequency adverbs (*sometimes, usually, often*) can come at the beginning of a sentence. For example: **Sometimes**, I go to bed at nine.
• In a negative sentence, the frequency adverb *usually* comes in front of the negative verb. For example: Stacy usually **doesn't** get up on time.

8 Practice

Read Nicole's e-mail to her e-pals. Then insert each adverb of frequency where appropriate.

Hi. I'm a senior in high school. My parents are very
always
strict. (1. always) They're on my case. (2. never) I can

stay late in school. (3. usually) After my last class, I go

straight home. (4. rarely) So I am part of any after-

school activity. (5. sometimes) My friends ask me to

hang out with them after school. (6. never) But I can do

that. I joined the Foreign Language Club. There's a

party at the club on Saturday, but I'm not sure I can go.

(7. rarely) My parents allow me to go to parties. What

should I do? I really want to go!

Nicole

9 Listening

🎧 **Listen to the conversation. Put a check (✔) in the correct box.**

1. Who's calling?
   ✔ Ms. Costa __ Mrs. Bryant __ Mr. Bryant

2. Who is she looking for?
   __ Tom __ Mr. Bryant __ Mrs. Bryant

3. Where is Mrs. Bryant?
   __ in Texas __ in Singapore __ in New York

4. What is Ms. Costa calling about?
   __ Tom's grades __ a party __ a meeting

5. What time should Tom be at the gym?
   __ at 4:00 __ at 3:00 __ at 5:00

10 Vocabulary

Teen activities

Complete the phrases below using the verbs in the box. One verb is used twice.

play	chat	read
watch	talk	listen to

1. ___play___ a musical instrument
2. _____ on the Internet
3. _____ TV
4. _____ video games
5. _____ music
6. _____ on the phone
7. _____ magazines

11 Reading

Before you read, discuss this question as a class: Why would a family move from a city to a rural area (countryside)?

Now read the article.

⪼The Family That Plays Together⪻

In the backwoods of Maine, a mother and her children wait outside their home for their father's return from work. Once their father is home, the family's musical ensemble is complete.

Sixteen-year-old Nick plays the viola; 13-year-old Zack is on the cello, and 12-year-old Bryanna plays the violin. Their mother, Whitney, runs the show. Their father, Shawn, is the teacher, conductor, and arranger. But the star of the family ensemble is 6-year-old Noah, who plays the piano. And he doesn't even read music yet!

Shawn believes that most children can do what his children are now doing. He has a good reason to believe that.

Four years ago in Chicago, none of his kids played music. Dinner conversations with his kids were always agonizing. All the kids talked about were video games. Both Whitney and Shawn decided it was time for a radical change. They headed out to the woods of Maine and replaced video games with musical instruments. Now in their new surroundings, the kids often play in the woods, bike, swim, build things, and then come back in and play their musical instruments.

After September 11, Shawn, a computer specialist, worked to help clear the World Trade Center site. He managed to come home for Thanksgiving to prepare for a charity concert to raise money for the children of Afghanistan. The family often performs at concerts around the world, including the Sydney Opera House in Australia, to raise money for poor countries.

According to Whitney, "[Music is] something that brings so much joy to so many people and it's something that we can do together....It has brought us together."

12 Comprehension

A. Work with a partner to guess the meaning of the underlined words in the reading. If you need help, use a dictionary.

B. Scan the article for the information that tells what each person in the family musical ensemble does. Write your answers in your notebook.

Example:

Whitney manages the family musical ensemble.

13 Your Turn

Discuss these questions in small groups:

1. Why did the family move to Maine?
2. Why is it better for them now?

14 Writing

In your notebook, answer these questions about yourself and your family.

1. What are you doing right now?
2. What activities do you and your family usually do together?

At the Party

🎧 Complete the story with sentences from the box. Then listen to check your answers.

It's OK, Justin.
She never really trusts me.
I'm getting it right now, Ms. Costa.
I heard that you usually don't go to parties.

1. Hi, Nicole. I'm glad you could come. (1) _____

No, I usually don't. Ms. Costa talked to my mom, so here I am.

Ms. Costa is cool.

2. Hey, you lovebirds. Are you enjoying yourselves?

Be quiet, Justin. You always say the wrong thing.

I'm just kidding. Sorry.

(2) _____

3. There you are, Justin. Where's that envelope?

Great. Thanks.

Ah! The yellow envelope, right? (3) _____

4. Nicole, your mom called. She wanted to know more about the party tonight.

I'm sorry. (4) _____

You're wrong, Nicole. She's just like all parents. Parents always worry about their children.

5. Thanks, Justin.

Here it is, Ms. Costa.

Could you give this letter to your mom?

Sure.

I wonder what's in this letter.

6.

2 It was quite an experience!

1 Reading

Read the postcards from Tom's mom.

Learning Goals

Communication
Make suggestions
Express preferences

Grammar
The simple past tense: regular and irregular verbs

Vocabulary
Review of common adjectives: antonyms

July 8, _____

My dear Nick and Tom,

Hi, guys. I'm taking a break from the conference. I picked up this beautiful postcard from a souvenir shop. I arrived at my hotel late last night. My flight was quite pleasant because the flight attendants were very efficient.

Singapore is very different from what I expected. The country is very small (it's about the size of a small city), very clean, and very rich! Everything runs like clockwork. I looked out my hotel window this morning to admire Singapore's skyline. I couldn't believe what I saw--lush green trees along the streets! I didn't see any brown leaves on the trees! I thought that was amazing.

Love,
Mom

Nicholas and Thomas Bryant
1450 Madison Street
San Antonio, TX   78204
U.S.A.

July 15, _____

Dear Ang San,

So, I'm back home in Texas. I just wanted to thank you and your wife for the wonderful time I had in Singapore. It was a busy but very interesting week, and I enjoyed my stay there. I especially loved the orchid garden. I had no idea there were so many varieties of orchids! And that breakfast at the zoo with Millie, the gentle gorilla, was quite an experience!

Best regards,
Emily Bryant

P.S. Thanks for telling me the secret behind those forever green trees!

Lim Ang San
900 Orange Grove Road
Singapore   258354

2 Comprehension

Write *T* for *true* or *F* for *false*. If the statement is false, correct the information to make the statement true.

  F   1. The postcards are from
     ~~Mrs.~~*Mrs.* ~~Mr.~~ Bryant.

_____ 2. Mrs. Bryant attended a conference.

_____ 3. Lim Ang San is from San Antonio.

_____ 4. Singapore is small but rich.

_____ 5. Millie is Mrs. Bryant's friend.

_____ 6. On July 15, Mrs. Bryant was still in Singapore.

3 Vocabulary

Write the words that mean the opposite of these adjectives from the postcards.

1. beautiful _____*ugly*_____

2. interesting _____

3. small _____

4. pleasant _____

5. efficient _____

6. rich _____

7. clean _____

8. busy _____

4 Pronunciation

Dropped vowels in middle syllables

🎧 **Listen and repeat. Circle the dropped vowel in each word.**

- int(e)resting
- favorite
- conference
- family
- preference

GRAMMAR FOCUS

The simple past tense: regular verbs

Affirmative statements
Mrs. Bryant **arrived** late last night.
She **traveled** to Singapore last week.

Negative statements
Mrs. Bryant **did not (didn't) arrive** early.
She **did not (didn't) travel** to Japan.

***Yes/No* questions**
Did Mrs. Bryant **arrive** late last night?

Short answers
Yes, she **did**. / No, she **didn't**.

Information questions
Who **did** she **visit** in Singapore?
When **did** she **arrive** in Singapore?

Short answers
Her business partners.
Late last night.

Remember! Some verbs change spelling when you add *-d* or *-ed*.
cry = cri**ed**   hug = hug**ged**   try = tri**ed**   prefer = prefer**red**

5 Practice

A. In your notebook, write *Yes/No* questions about the information on the postcards. Use the cues below.

1. pick up *Did Mrs. Bryant pick up the postcard*
    from a souvenir shop?

2. arrive
3. look out
4. enjoy
5. love

B. In your notebook, rewrite your *Yes/No* questions from Exercise A into information questions. Use the cues below.

1. Where *Where did Mrs. Bryant pick up the*
    postcard from?

2. When
3. Why
4. What
5. What

The simple past tense: irregular verbs

Affirmative statements

Mrs. Bryant **went** back home to Texas.

She **had** a wonderful time in Singapore.

Her hosts **took** her to the orchid garden.

Yes/No question

Did Mrs. Bryant **go** back home to Texas?

Information questions

Where **did** Mrs. Bryant **have** breakfast?

When **did** Mrs. Bryant **go** back home to Texas?

Negative statements

Mrs. Bryant **did not go** on a vacation.

She **did not have** a lot of luggage.

Her hosts **did not take** her to a museum.

Short answer

Yes, she **did**. / No, she **didn't**.

Short answers

At the zoo. (She **had** breakfast at the zoo.)

On July 14. (She **went** back home to Texas on July 14.)

Remember! • Learn the simple past tense forms of irregular verbs by heart.

go—went   have—had   take—took

• Contraction: did not = didn't

6 Practice

Have a competition! Go to page 88.

7 Writing

Write a short paragraph about Mrs. Bryant's trip to Singapore on the stationery below. Use the information in the postcards. Use both regular and irregular verbs.

Example:

Mrs. Bryant was in Singapore last week. She

attended a conference...

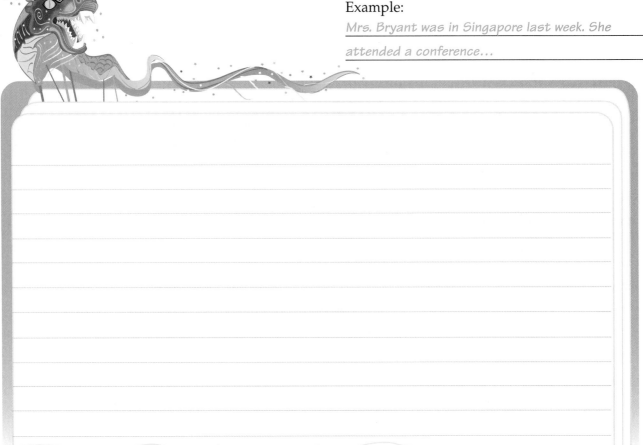

8 Dialogue

🎧 **Read and listen.**

Stacy: That was a fun party last Saturday.

Justin: Yeah, it was. But why did Ms. Costa keep asking me to do things for her?

Tom: To keep you out of trouble, I guess.

Justin: Ha, ha. Anyway, why don't we do something together this weekend?

Steve: I know. There's a wildlife exhibit at the Witte Museum.

Stacy: Wildlife? You mean snakes? No way. I'd rather watch TV. I hate snakes.

Tom: Why don't we watch a show at the IMAX theater?

Steve: Nah, I don't feel like going to the theater. I'd rather be outside.

Justin: Jeez. You guys are difficult.

Stacy: How about going to the River Walk? We can just hang out there.

Tom: That's a great idea! Umm, Nicole? Are you all right?

Nicole: Huh? Oh. I'm OK. But I can't hang out with you guys this weekend.

9 Comprehension

Read each question. Circle the correct letter.

1. Who kept Justin busy at the party?
   a. Mrs. Bryant   b. Ms. Costa   c. Mr. Bryant
2. What place does Steve suggest?
   a. the Witte Museum   b. the IMAX theater
   c. the River Walk
3. Who doesn't like snakes?
   a. Steve   b. Stacy   c. Tom
4. Who doesn't feel like watching a show?
   a. Steve   b. Justin   c. Nicole
5. Who can't go with the group?
   a. Stacy   b. Tom   c. Nicole

10 Communication

Making suggestions; expressing preferences

🎧 **Read and listen. Then role-play the conversation using places in your town.**

A: Hey, why don't we go to the movies?

B: No, I don't feel like going to the movies. I'd rather just hang out.

A: How about going to the Japanese Tea Garden?

B: That's a great idea!

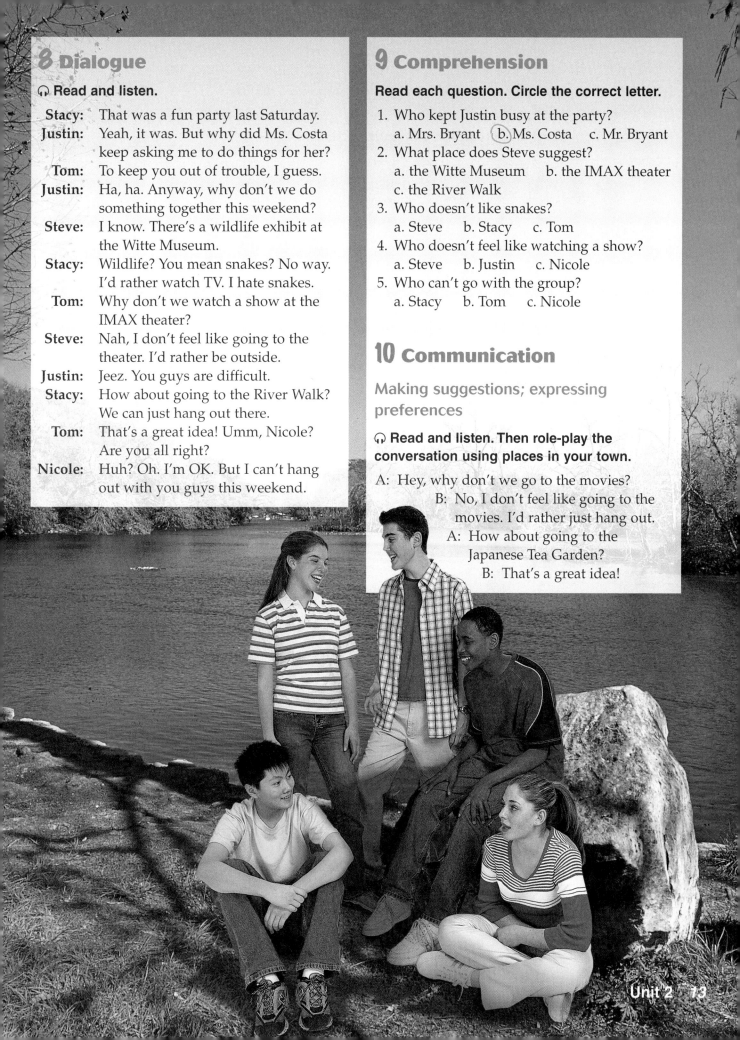

11 Reading

With your class, discuss what you know about San Antonio's history and places of interest.

Now read about some of San Antonio's interesting places.

San Antonio—Past and Present

The Spanish missions, including the Alamo, formed the foundation for the city of San Antonio. From a small settlement near the missions, San Antonio grew to become the ninth largest city in the United States.

The Alamo

In 1836, 189 Texas soldiers fell at the Alamo when they finally lost their battle against Mexican General Santa Anna's army. Today, a chapel and a museum remind us of that historic event.

Mission Trails

Spain extended its territory from Mexico by setting up missions in Concepcion, San Jose, San Juan, and Espada. Often, these missions had to be protected by forts.

River Walk

River Walk, found in downtown San Antonio, is the pride of the city. Lush green trees such as cypresses, oaks, and willows line the banks of the San Antonio River. Along the walkways are restaurants, shops, and nightclubs.

Market Square (*El Mercado*)

The Market Square resembles an authentic Mexican market and offers 32 shops. The square is usually the scene of Hispanic festivals, with food, *mariachi* music, and Mexican dances.

12 Comprehension

Answer the following questions orally.

1. Where is the Alamo?

   It's in San Antonio, Texas.

2. What is the Alamo?
3. How did Spain extend its territory from Mexico?
4. Where is River Walk?
5. What is *El Mercado*? What happens there?

13 Writing

In your notebook, write a paragraph about a historical place in your city. Explain why it is a good place to visit on vacation.

Progress Check *Units 1 and 2*

Grammar

A. Fill in the blanks with either the simple present or the present continuous tense. Use the cues. (2 points each)

1. Oh, no. It *(rain)* _is raining_ outside. It always _rains_ at this time.

2. Look at her. She *(sleep)* _____. She usually _____ in math class.

3. We *(take)* _____ a break right now. We rarely _____ breaks, but work is slow today.

4. Ray *(scratch)* _____ his head. He usually _____ his head when he doesn't know the answer.

5. The phone *(ring)* _____. I wonder who it is. My phone rarely _____.

6. Liza *(erase)* _____ the board again. She always _____ the board before we get a chance to take notes.

B. Rewrite the sentences using the simple past tense. Use the cues. (3 points each)

1. My parents travel every summer.
   (last summer) _They traveled last summer._

2. Rose works on weekends.
   (last weekend) _____

3. My brother usually cries at the doctor's office.
   (this morning) _____

4. We always have company on Fridays.
   (last Friday) _____

5. The children usually do their homework before dinner.
   (last night) _____

Vocabulary

C. Match the verbs with the phrases. Write the correct letters. (1 point each)

_c_ 1. talk   a. the guitar

____ 2. read   b. a show

____ 3. hang out   c. on the phone

____ 4. listen to   d. on the Internet

____ 5. play   e. the newspaper

____ 6. watch   f. with friends

____ 7. chat   g. the radio

D. Write words that mean the opposite of the adjectives below. Choose words from the box. (1 point each)

dirty	inefficient	big	ugly
boring	unpleasant	slow	poor

1. efficient _inefficient_   5. busy _____

2. interesting _____   6. clean _____

3. beautiful _____   7. rich _____

4. small _____   8. pleasant _____

Communication

E. Write three sentences introducing yourself to your new class. Include your name, your grade, your age, and the foreign language you are studying. (3 points)

_____

_____

_____

F. Write a dialogue. Student A suggests that Student B hang out at his or her house. Student B says "no" and tells Student A what he or she would prefer to do. (3 points)

A: _____

B: _____

Wide Angle on the world

1 Reading

A. Read the article on parents and teens.

B. Answer the following questions in your notebook.

1. What are three assumptions that parents usually make about their teenaged children?
2. What is one reason parents make these assumptions about teenagers?
3. What advice does the writer give to parents?
4. What advice does the writer give to teenagers?

2 Listening

**A. ⌒ Listen to the radio show "Teen Talk."
Then circle the letter next to each correct response.**

1. Sean is _____.
   - a. sociable
   - (b.) a loner
   - c. athletic

2. He likes to _____.
   - a. read
   - b. play sports
   - c. hang out

3. Katrina is _____.
   - a. athletic
   - b. fashionable
   - c. lazy

4. She likes _____.
   - a. clothes
   - b. hanging out
   - c. sports

5. Cathy is _____.
   - a. a loner
   - b. fashionable
   - c. athletic

6. She likes _____.
   - a. basketball
   - b. reading
   - c. teen fashion

B. Listen to the talk show again. Then discuss these questions as a class.

1. What problem does each teenager on the radio program have with his or her parents?
2. Do you think that the host understands both the parents and the teenagers? Support your answer with examples from the radio host's responses.

3 Speaking

Work with a small group. Discuss these questions.

1. What should teenagers do so that their parents won't worry about them?
2. What should parents do to avoid conflicts with teenagers?
3. Should parents tell teenagers what kinds of friends to have or what kinds of clothes to wear? Explain.

PARENTS and TEENS: Living with Each Other

By Suki Asato, Age 17

Conflicts between parents and teenagers are common, mainly because parents make assumptions[1] about their teens that often do not prove true. Look at these popular assumptions that parents sometimes make.

One: Usually, when their teenagers have wild friends, parents immediately think that their teenagers will act the same way. This assumption, though, does not often prove true. Of course, there are some teens who are easily influenced by their friends, but there are many teens who follow their parents' guidelines and rules no matter what their friends do.

Two: Parents usually have problems with teens' appearance. They think that there is a connection between the clothes and hairstyles that teens wear and the way these teens behave. Again, this assumption often does not prove true. There are many fine[2] teenagers who have pink hair and who dress like rock stars.

Three: Parents may assume that they have all the answers to teens' problems and that they know exactly what teens are going through because they were teenagers once. But this assumption also does not always prove true. Parents forget that each generation of teenagers has different problems.

Parents make these assumptions about their teens because they love them, care about them, and worry about them. And teens give their parents plenty of things to worry about! But if these assumptions don't help either parents or teens, then what can?

Parents and teens need to communicate better with each other. Instead of shouting at their teens when they are worried about them, parents need to be open, accepting, and understanding. Teens, on the other hand, should not be afraid to talk to their parents. They need to approach their parents as the loving, caring people they are. After all, recent surveys indicate that many parents today are understanding, accepting, and yes, even cool!

1. **assumption:** something that you think is true even though there is no proof
2. **fine:** good and honest; decent

3 Do I have to?

Learning Goals

Communication
Talk about obligations

Grammar
Have to: simple present and simple past forms

Vocabulary
Household chores

1 Vocabulary

Write sentences that describe what the people in the pictures are doing. Use phrases from the box.

do the laundry	clear the table	cook lunch (or dinner)
do the grocery shopping	iron the clothes	wash (or do) the dishes
vacuum the floor	make the bed	clean the room

1. *She's making the bed.*

2. _____

3. _____

4. _____

5. _____

6. _____

7. _____

8. _____

9. _____

GRAMMAR FOCUS

Have to: simple present

Affirmative statements
Stacy **has to clean** her room.
The boys **have to clean** their room.

Yes/No **questions**
Does Stacy **have to clean** her room?
Does Tom **have to clean** his room?

Negative statements
Tom **doesn't have to clean** his room.
The girls **don't have to clean** their room.

Short answers
Yes, she **does**. / No, she **doesn't**.
Yes, he **does**. / No, he **doesn't**.

Remember! *Have to* expresses necessity and obligation.

2 Pronunciation

Reduced forms: *have to* and *has to*

⌒ **Listen and repeat.**

/hæv ta/ (hafta)
• I have to go.
• We have to meet later.

/hæz ta/ (hasta)
• He has to try harder.
• Carla has to finish her project.

3 Practice

A. Read the note below. In your notebook, write sentences telling what Brad and Tracy have to do this weekend.

Example:

Brad has to clear the table after breakfast.

B. Answer the questions using the note in Exercise A.

1. Do Tracy and Brad have to do their chores this weekend?
   Yes, they do.

2. Does Brad have to do the laundry?
   _____

3. Does he have to make the beds?
   _____

4. Does Tracy have to vacuum the floor?
   _____

5. Does she have to clean the bedrooms?
   _____

Brad and Tracy,
   I have to work this weekend. Make sure you do your chores before you go out.

Brad, here are your chores:
1. clear the table after breakfast
2. do the dishes
3. do the laundry
4. vacuum the floor

And Tracy, here are yours:
1. make the beds
2. clean the bedrooms
3. go to the supermarket with Dad
4. make dinner

Mom

4 Listening

🎧 **Brad and Tracy are complaining. Listen to their phone conversation with their mom. Then answer the questions using complete sentences.**

1. What are Brad and Tracy complaining about?

    They're complaining about their chores.

2. Where does Tracy have to be this afternoon?

    _____

3. Where does Brad have to go this morning?

    _____

4. What time does Tracy have to be at the party?

    _____

5. What two things does Tracy have to do before the party?

    _____

6. Who doesn't have to do the chores this Saturday?

    _____

5 Your Turn

What about you? What do you have to do on weekends? In your notebook, list at least three chores. Then, using your list, tell a partner what you have to do on weekends.

Example:

1. *Do the dishes:*

    On Saturdays, I usually have to do the dishes.

 GRAMMAR FOCUS

Have to: simple past

Affirmative statement	**Negative statement**
Tracy **had to clean** her bedroom last Saturday.	Brad **didn't have to do** his chores last Saturday.
Yes/No question	**Short answers**
Did Tracy **have to do** her chores?	Yes, she **did**. / No, she **didn't**.
Information question	**Answer**
What **did** Brad and Tracy **have to do** last weekend?	They **had to do** their chores.

Remember! *Had to* is the simple past form of *have to*.

6 Practice

A. Fill in the blanks with the simple past form of *have to*.

Megan: Hey, Kevin. You missed my party last weekend.

Kevin: I know. I (1) <u>had to</u> work.

Megan: Why (2) _____ you _____ work? Wasn't it your day off?

Kevin: I'm on call at Party City. Somebody called in sick, so I (3) _____ fill in for the person.

Megan: I hate it when people call in sick. What (4) _____ you _____ do at Party City last weekend?

Kevin: I (5) _____ unpack all the fall costumes that arrived.

Megan: That doesn't seem too difficult.

Kevin: You haven't heard it all.

Megan: What else (6) _____ you _____ do?

Kevin: You won't believe this. It's the fall season, right? So I (7) _____ stand out on the street holding up the sign "Have a party at Party City."

Megan: Oh, no. (8) _____ you _____ wear a costume?

Kevin: You bet, I did. I (9) _____ wear a pumpkin costume. I'm never going back there.

B. Work with a partner. Take turns asking and answering *Yes/No* questions, using the dialogue in Exercise A.

Example:

Did Kevin have to work last weekend?

Yes, he did.

C. Write three information questions about the dialogue in Exercise A. Use the cues and *have to*. Then answer the questions.

1. (What) *What did Kevin have to do last weekend?*

    He had to work at Party City.

2. (Where) _____

    _____

3. (Why) _____

    _____

4. (What) _____

    _____

7 Reading

Before you read, discuss this question as a class: Should children and teens help out with household chores? Why or why not?

Now read the article.

Crosstalk
Parents vs. Kids

AMY

I think household chores are a pain. Every day after breakfast, I have to clear the table. On weekends, I have to clean the bathroom and do the dishes after dinner. There are two things that I hate most in life—cleaning the bathroom and doing the dishes.

My mom says my bedroom is a mess. I don't think it's really that messy. OK, there are some clothes on the floor, but it's *my* bedroom. Mom doesn't have to look at it if it bothers her. But she just has to check my room every day and nag me to clean up "this mess!" Of course, I promise her each time that I will clean it up— when I have the time.

My brother, Mark, doesn't have to do very much at home. Sometimes, he helps Dad wash the car and water the plants. Those are not difficult chores at all. I usually have to remind him to help me do the laundry, but after he puts the laundry in the washer, he runs back to his computer.

AMY'S MOM

I'm a working mother with two kids. I cook, do the laundry, iron the clothes, do the grocery shopping, etc. I don't mind housework on weekends, but during the work week? I ask my daughter, Amy, to help me with the chores. But I always have to ask her three or four times. She often pretends not to hear me, or she goes off in a huff.

Her bedroom is a mess! There is dirty laundry, stale food, used dishes, and unwashed socks and sneakers all over the room.

Amy complains about her brother Mark. Mark is only a child, so he does only small chores. I worry about Amy. She's 14, and she has to learn to help out with the housework. What is she going to be like when she's older?

8 Comprehension

In your notebook, complete the following activities.

1. Make a list of Amy's chores; then list Mark's chores.
2. List two complaints Amy has about her mom.
3. List two complaints Amy's mom has about Amy.

9 Writing

Write a paragraph about your responsibilities at home. Use the questions that follow to help you.

1. What do you have to do at home?
2. Do you like your chores? What don't you like about your chores?
3. Does each member of your family have chores? Is the distribution of chores fair? Why or why not?

10 Speaking

Work with a group of five students. Share your paragraph from Exercise 9 with your group. Ask other students questions about their chores at home.

Explaining to Tom

🎧 **Listen and read. Then, as a class, discuss this question: What advice would you give Tom about his situation with Nicole?**

1

Hi, Nicole.

Oh, hi, Tom. What are you doing here?

2

I'm waiting for you.

Why? You don't have to do that.

3

I know. Look, Nicole. I just want us to be friends. Why are you avoiding me?

Umm. . . Excuse me. I have to get this call.

4

Hello? Yes, I'm on my way. Yes. I'll be there in half an hour. Bye.

5

Look, Tom, I really have to go. Can we talk about this later?

6

OK. Can I call you at home?

Well. . . no, please don't. That call was from my dad, and I have to go home now. Bye.

4

Who's going to the game?

Learning Goals

Communication
Express future plans

Grammar
The present continuous to express future time
Verb + infinitive

Vocabulary
Sports and sports locations

1 Dialogue

⌒ Listen and read.

Justin: Who's coming with me to the soccer game on Friday night?

Steve: I'd love to go, but I'm not spending $70 on a ticket. I don't have that kind of money.

Stacy: Me neither. How about you, Tom? Are you going with Justin?

Tom: I can't. I don't have any money either.

Justin: Well, consider me your hero. I have four free tickets from my father's office.

Tom: Cool!

Stacy: Count me out. I need to finish my history project this weekend.

Justin: That means we have one extra ticket. Do you think Nicole would like to come?

Tom: No. She's not into sports.

Steve: OK. So, when and where are we meeting?

2 Comprehension

Write the name or names. Who. . .

1. has tickets? ___Justin___

2. doesn't have any money?

   _____

3. doesn't like sports? _____

4. is going to the game? _____

3 Useful Phrases

⌒ Listen and repeat.

- Me neither.
- Consider me your hero.
- Count me out.
- She's not into sports.

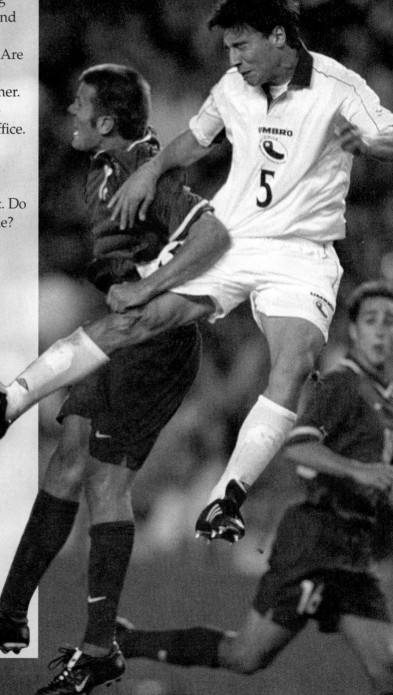

GRAMMAR FOCUS

The present continuous to express future time

Affirmative statements

Stacy **is staying** home Friday night.

The boys **are going** to the game.

Yes/No questions

Is Stacy **staying** home?

Are the boys **going** to the game?

Information questions

What **is** Stacy **doing**?

Where **are** the boys **going**?

Negative statements

Stacy **is not going** out Friday night.

The girls **are not going** out Friday night.

Short answers

Yes, she **is**. / No, she **isn't**.

Yes, they **are**. / No, they **aren't**.

Answers

She**'s staying** home.

They**'re going** to a soccer game.

Remember! Use the present continuous to express future plans that are definite.

4 Practice

In pairs, use the itinerary below to ask and answer at least four questions about Sally and Tina's vacation. Use contractions.

Example:

What are Sally and Tina doing on Sunday morning?

They're flying to Frankfurt.

JULY

Sunday 1 Fly to Frankfurt early in the morning; arrive in Frankfurt in the evening

Monday 2 Tour Frankfurt; go to Mainz; take a boat cruise along the Main River; take the night train to Berlin

Tuesday 3 Visit the Berlin Wall, Checkpoint Charlie Museum, etc.; buy souvenirs; take the night train back to Frankfurt

Wednesday 4 Fly to Paris (4 A.M.); take a walking tour of city (2 P.M.)

Thursday 5

Friday 6

Saturday 7

5 Listening

A. 🎧 **Listen and complete the itinerary in Exercise 4. Choose from the phrases below.**

- spend the night in London
- tour London
- take the night train to London
- go up the Eiffel Tower
- visit the Louvre
- leave for home from London

B. In your notebook, write sentences about what Sally and Tina are doing for the rest of the week.

On Thursday, Sally and Tina are...

6 Communication

Expressing future plans

🎧 **Listen and read. Then role-play a similar conversation.**

A: What are you doing Sunday?

B: I'm going shopping. Why?

A: How about coming to the baseball game with us?

B: Great! When and where are you meeting?

A: Outside the mall at 3 P.M.

B. Cool. See you then.

Communicating with Your Friends

How well do you communicate with your friends? Take this test to find out. Complete each question by circling the letter next to your response.

1. Your friends want to go swimming this weekend, but you hate swimming. You'd prefer to go bike riding. Do you . . .

a. agree to go but forget to bring your swimsuit?

b. try to persuade them to go bike riding instead?

c. decide to tell them you hate swimming and then wait for their response?

2. Some friends are planning to go ice-skating. They ask you to go. You can't ice-skate, but you really want to go. Do you . . .

a. agree to go, and hope to find an ice-skating instructor at the rink?

b. agree to go, and try to learn to skate on your own, but give up?

c. decide to tell your friends you can't skate, but you'd still like to go with them?

3. Your friend had promised to get you tickets for an important baseball game for your birthday. Your friend is sorry, but he can't afford to pay for the tickets now. You are disappointed. Do you . . .

a. refuse to accept your friend's apology?

b. pretend to not be upset?

c. accept the apology, and offer to pay for both tickets yourself?

Your Score and Rating

To find out your score, give yourself one point for each *a* response you circled, two points for each *b* response, and three points for each *c* response. Then add up your points and read your rating below.

Nine points: Congratulations! You're a model for communicating well with friends.

Six–eight points: Most of the time you communicate well with your friends.

Three–five points: Oops! You need to improve how you communicate with your friends.

GRAMMAR FOCUS

Verb + infinitive

Jill **wants to see** the new house.
My parents **offered to help** me.
These verbs can be followed by an infinitive:

can't afford	hope	refuse
agree	learn	try
begin	need	can't wait
decide	offer	want
fail	plan	would like
forget	promise	would prefer

Remember! In a negative statement, *not* goes between the verb and the infinitive. For example: He decided **not** to go.

7 Practice

Complete the ads. Fill in the blanks with the appropriate infinitives. Choose the verbs from the box.

practice	receive	correspond	hear
learn	answer	exchange	

Tomsk Polytechnic, Russia
I'm a teacher at the Polytechnic. My students would like *(1)* _to exchange_ e-mails with students from around the world. Their first language is Russian, so they need *(2)* _____ their English with other students. They promise *(3)* _____ all e-mails in English. They hope *(4)* _____ about other cultures through the e-mails. Please write soon.
Svetlana Kazarina
English Teacher

El Pilar, Spain
My students are in junior high school. My students like sports, especially football and golf. They would love *(5)* _____ with other students. They can't wait *(6)* _____ e-mails from other countries. We hope *(7)* _____ from students from around the world.
Eva Santillan
English Teacher

8 Vocabulary

Sports and sports locations

A. Write the name of the sport below each picture.

basketball	tennis	volleyball	soccer
swimming	running	baseball	golf

1. _____tennis_____

2. _____

3. _____

4. _____

5. _____

6. _____

7. _____

8. _____

B. Match the sports and the sports locations. Write the letters. (Some items will have the same answer.)

_d_ 1. basketball	a. field
___ 2. swimming	b. course
___ 3. baseball	c. track
___ 4. volleyball	d. court
___ 5. golf	e. pool
___ 6. running	
___ 7. tennis	
___ 8. soccer	

9 Reading

Read these facts about golf champion Tiger Woods.

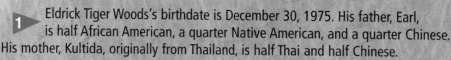

Facts you didn't know about Tiger Woods

1. Eldrick Tiger Woods's birthdate is December 30, 1975. His father, Earl, is half African American, a quarter Native American, and a quarter Chinese. His mother, Kultida, originally from Thailand, is half Thai and half Chinese.

2. His father is a retired lieutenant colonel in the U.S. army.

3. His father decided to call his son Tiger after a Vietnamese soldier called Nguyen "Tiger" Phong. Phong saved Earl's life in Vietnam twice.

4. At six months, Tiger loved to watch his father practice his swings into a net in his garage. Even at that age, Tiger tried to imitate his father's swing.

5. At the age of two, Tiger won an under-10 competition at the Navy Club.

6. By the age of five, Tiger was regularly scoring in the 90s around 18-hole golf courses. As a result, he was invited to appear on a TV program called *That's Incredible*.

7. Tiger was 13 when he received a letter from Wally Goodwin, a golf coach at Stanford University. The letter began, "Here at Stanford, I'm finding that it is never too early to get word out to you exceptional young men …"

8. On August 28, 1996, Tiger decided to turn pro. He started his pro career with a $40 million endorsement deal from Nike. But he couldn't afford to pay the $100 entry fee at the Greater Milwaukee Open. The golf champion with a $40 million endorsement had only $10 in his pocket at the time!

10 Comprehension

A. Scan the reading in Exercise 9 to find the infinitives. Circle them.

B. You have three minutes to do this task. Scan the reading to answer the items below.

1. Tiger Woods's birthdate. _December 30, 1975_
2. His father's name. _____
3. His father's occupation. _____
4. His mother's native country. _____
5. The name of the Vietnamese soldier who saved Earl Woods's life during the Vietnam War. _____
6. The TV program five-year-old Tiger appeared in. _____
7. The university that recruited Tiger when he was 13. _____

11 Writing and Speaking

A. Using the information in the reading in Exercise 9, write five interview questions for Tiger Woods in your notebook. Use infinitives in some of your questions.

Example:

Why did your father decide to call you "Tiger"?

B. Work with a partner. Pretend that you are a journalist and your partner is Tiger Woods. Interview your partner, using your questions from Exercise A. Have your partner respond using information from the reading.

Journalist: Why did your father decide to call you "Tiger"?

Woods: He called me Tiger after a Vietnamese soldier named Nguyen "Tiger" Phong, who saved his life in Vietnam.

Progress Check *Units 3 and 4*

Grammar

A. Fill in the blanks with the present continuous form to express definite future plans. (1 point each)

1. *(come)* ___Are___ you ___coming___ to my party next Saturday?
2. No, I'm not. I *(visit)* _____ my grandmother next Saturday.
3. We *(not/travel)* _____ at all next summer.
4. My parents *(arrive)* _____ home tonight from a business trip.
5. My brother *(meet)* _____ them at the airport at midnight.
6. *(join)* _____ Ken _____ our study group this weekend?
7. Yes, he is, but he *(come)* _____ later.

B. Fill in the blanks with the infinitive of the verb in parentheses. (1 point each)

1. Would you like *(sit)* _____ with me?
2. We can't wait *(see)* _____ our report cards.
3. Why do you always refuse *(come)* _____ with me?
4. My family plans *(invite)* _____ your family for Christmas.
5. I want *(finish)* _____ my work before the end of summer.

Vocabulary

C. Complete the phrases. Write the appropriate verb from the box. *Do* can be used twice. (1 point each)

make clear do vacuum clean iron

1. ___clean___ the bathroom
2. _____ the floor
3. _____ the laundry
4. _____ the beds
5. _____ the clothes
6. _____ the dishes
7. _____ the dining table

D. Complete the sentences. Write the appropriate sports locations from the box. (1 point each)

court field track course pool

1. We swim in a ___pool___.
2. The Williams sisters play tennis on a tennis _____.
3. Tiger Woods plays golf on a golf _____.
4. Michael Johnson runs on a _____.
5. Soccer is played on a soccer _____.

Communication

E. Write a dialogue about next weekend. Ask what your friend's plans are and invite him or her to go out with you. (5 points)

Example:
A: What are you doing next weekend?
B: Nothing much. I'm catching up on my project. How about you?
A: I'm . . .

A: _____

_____

B: _____

_____

A: _____

_____

B: _____

_____

SONG

Marc Anthony

Marc Anthony was born in New York City in 1968. He started singing when he was very young, and he began writing songs when he was in high school. His big break came in 1997, when he won a Grammy award for *Contra La Corriente* (*Against the Current*).

I Need To Know

They say around the way you've asked for me
There's even talk about you wanting me
I must admit that's what I want to hear
But that's just talk until you take me there

Chorus

If it's true don't leave me all alone out here
Wondering if you're ever going to take me there
Tell me what you're feeling 'cause I need to know
Girl you got to let me know which way to go

I need to know
I need to know
Tell me baby girl 'cause I need to know
I need to know
I need to know
Tell me baby girl 'cause I need to know

My every thought is of this being true
It's getting harder not to think of you
Girl I'm exactly where I want to be
The only thing's I need you here with me

Repeat chorus two times

1. 🎧 Listen to the song. How many times do you hear the phrase, "I need to know"?

2. What does the narrator want the girl to tell him? Why do you think so?

3. In your notebook, write a short e-mail to a friend about something you really want to do. Use the words below and your imagination.

need to	want to	have to

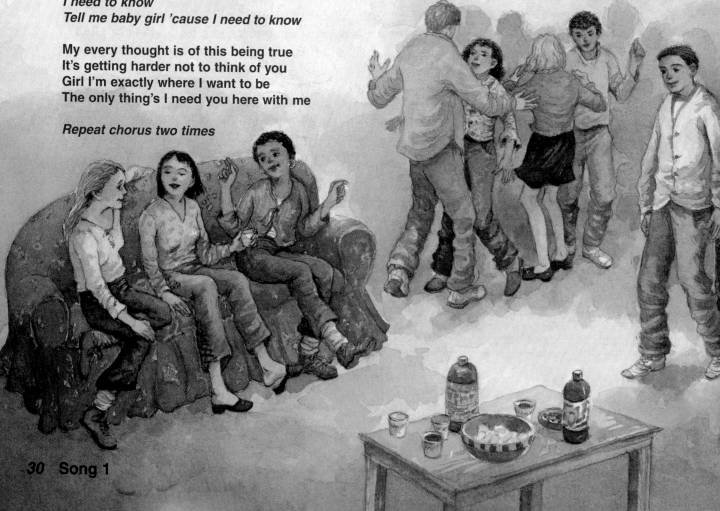

GAME *Mystery Celebrity*

Steps

1. Play this game in groups of six or more.

2. One person thinks of a famous living person. He or she can start with a celebrity on this page.

3. The person says the first letter of the celebrity's first name. The other players take turns asking *Yes/No* questions about the celebrity.

4. Each player keeps asking until he or she gets a *No* answer. Then that player is out of the game.

5. The player who guesses the name correctly is the winner. The winner thinks of the next mystery celebrity.

5 I'll have a sandwich.

Learning Goals

Communication
Order food items and drinks

Grammar
Will and *won't* for decisions, promises, and future predictions
The imperative

Vocabulary
Food items and drinks
Dance and exercise verbs

1 Vocabulary

Food items and drinks

Write the names of the food items and drinks under the correct category below.

MENU

Soups

Salads

Entrées (Main Course)

Desserts

Drinks

New York steak
soda
cheesecake
pudding
chicken noodle soup
grilled chicken
milk
pasta special
chocolate cake
onion soup
orange juice
bottled water
ice cream
tomato soup
Greek salad
seafood platter
vegetable soup
mixed green salad

2 Pronunciation

The sounds /tʃ/ and /dʒ/

A. ⌂ Listen and repeat.

/tʃ/	/dʒ/
choose	**j**uice
cheese	**j**erky
chicken	**g**ee
lun**ch**	**G**eorge
sandwi**ch**	fu**dge**
wat**ch**	langua**ge**

B. ⌂ Listen. Then write the sound you hear, tʃ or dʒ in the blanks.

_tʃ_ 1. I'd like some cheese in my sandwich, please.

____ 2. She likes jelly but not jam.

____ 3. We'll have some juice and ice cream with hot fudge.

____ 4. My brother shouldn't use teen language at his age.

____ 5. You may choose from this lunch menu.

3 Dialogue

🎧 **Listen and read.**

Stacy: Come on, you guys! You're taking forever to decide. Nicole has to be home by seven.

Steve: OK. OK. Where's the server?

Stacy: There she is. Miss!

Server: Hello. Are you all ready to order?

Stacy: Uh-huh.

Steve: I'll have the mixed green salad and the New York steak, umm, medium-rare. And a large soda, please. Oh, wait. Will that take a long time?

Server: No, it won't.

Nicole: Don't worry, we'll have enough time. A small Greek salad for me, please. Oh, and I'll have a small soda.

Tom: Is that all? Wow! I'll have the pasta special and a large soda.

Stacy: And I'll have a small green salad, the grilled chicken, and bottled water.

Server: Thanks. I'll be right back with your orders.

Stacy: Great!

Justin: Umm, Miss, what about me? I still need to order . . .

4 Comprehension

Write the names of the food items and drinks each person orders.

Steve	Nicole	Tom	Stacy
mixed green salad			
New York steak			
large soda			

5 Useful Phrases

🎧 **Listen and repeat. Then match the sentences that mean the same thing. Write the letters.**

_b_ 1. Come on, you guys!

____ 2. You're taking forever.

____ 3. Is that all?

____ 4. What about me?

a. You forgot me.

b. Hurry up, everyone.

c. You're really slow.

d. That's not enough.

GRAMMAR FOCUS

Will and won't for decisions and promises

Affirmative statements	Negative statements
I'll **have** a salad.	I **won't** have a salad.
I'll **be** right back with your orders.	I **won't** be long.

6 Practice

Complete the dialogue with the correct forms of will + have or won't + have.

Stacy: Tom and I will be right back. Order something for us, OK?

Justin: I (1) <u>'ll have</u> the pudding, and Stacy (2) _____ ice cream. Chocolate ice cream, please.

Nicole: Tom (3) _____ cheesecake.

Steve: No, he (4) _____ cheesecake! He hates it!

Nicole: OK. OK. Tom (5) _____ ice cream, too. With hot fudge!

Steve: That's better! And I (6) _____ chocolate cake. And milk.

Server: And for you, miss?

Nicole: I (7) _____ any dessert, thanks. I have to go home now.

GRAMMAR FOCUS

Will and won't for future predictions

Yes/No questions	Short answers
Will that **take** a long time?	Yes, it **will**./No, it **won't**.
Will Nicole **be** home in time?	Yes, she **will**./No, she **won't**.
Will there **be** lots of people at the party?	Yes, there **will**./No, there **won't**.

Information questions	Short answers
Where **will** they **have** dinner?	At Max's Diner.
When **will** Nicole **be** home?	By seven.

7 Practice

In your notebook, write five *Yes/No* questions about what will happen this weekend. Then ask and answer the questions with a partner.

Examples:
A: Will you be at the party on Friday night?
B: Yes, I will. *OR*
No, I won't.

A: Will there be food at the party on Friday night?
B: Yes, there will. *OR*
No, there won't.

8 Information Gap

Student A, go to page 91.
Student B, go to page 92.
Follow the instructions.

9 Communication

Ordering food items and drinks

🎧 **Listen. Then role-play the conversation.**

A: Are you ready to order?
B: No, not yet. Could you give us a few minutes, please?
A: Sure. Take your time.

(Later)
B: Miss, we're ready to order.
A: OK. What will it be?
B: I'll have the pasta special and a large soda, please.
C: And I'll have the grilled chicken and a bottled water.

GRAMMAR FOCUS

The imperative

Affirmative statements	Negative statements
Stand up. / **Look out!**	**Don't stand up.**
Please **close** the door.	Please **don't close** the door.
Walk three blocks.	**Don't turn** right.

> **Remember!** • Use the imperative to (1) give a command, (2) make a polite request, or (3) give directions.
> • The base form of the verb is used in the imperative. The negative form is formed from *don't* + the base form of the verb.

---

10 Practice

Look at the map below. In your notebook, write directions for Nicole and Stacy, telling them how to get from the post office to the shopping mall. Use the expressions below.

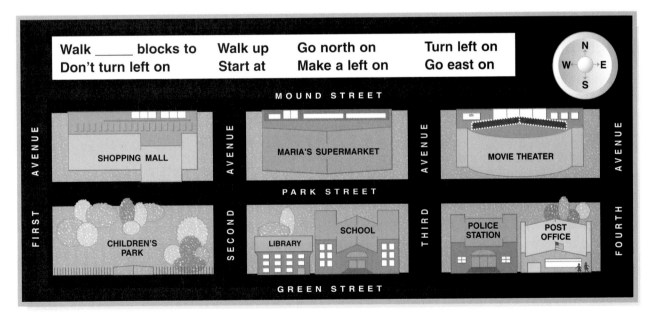

---

11 Practice

Have a competition! Go to page 88.

12 Vocabulary

Dance and exercise verbs

hop	turn	spin
shake	stomp	step up
slide	kick	rock

Write the correct verb on the line below each picture.

① _____kick_____

② _____

③ _____

④ _____

⑤ _____

⑥ _____

⑦ _____

⑧ _____

⑨ _____

13 Listening

🎧 **Listen to the dance video instructions. Number the steps in the order in which they are given. Then demonstrate the steps to a classmate.**

_____ Stomp with your left foot.

_____ Walk back four times!

_____ Do the box step on the spot.

__1__ Clap your hands!

_____ Stomp with your right foot.

_____ Slide to the left.

_____ Hop forward.

14 Your Turn

Work with a partner. Discuss the questions below. Try to use the verbs from Exercise 12.

1. Do you like to dance? Why or why not?
2. What is your favorite dance move? Tell your partner about it.

Learn to Learn

Listening to native speakers of English to improve pronunciation

Listening to native speakers of English can help you improve your pronunciation in English. Try to watch and listen to exercise and dance videos in English. Focus on specific sounds that you want to learn, for example, the sound /st/ in *stomp* and *step up*. Keep repeating words with those specific sounds.

All About Nicole

I'll have to check with my parents.
Not that good,
I have to go.
It'll be OK. You'll see.
would you like to come
they aren't so bad.

A. 🎧 **Before you listen, complete the conversation with the items from the box. Then listen to check your answers.**

1. These tutoring classes with the kids are fun. Hey, how are you and Nicole doing?

(1) _____ Stacy. She never wants to hang out with me.

2. Don't worry, Tom. (2) _____

Thanks, Stacy. . . . Oh, (3) _____ My kids are waiting.

3. So, what's the matter with Tom?

He's upset because Nicole always avoids him.

I think she's afraid to tell her parents about him. But (4) _____ We're neighbors, you know.

4. Hi, Nicole. How are your kids?

They're great. Look at their drawings!

They're terrific. By the way, (5) _____ to my house after this?

I'm not sure. (6) _____

5. Why doesn't Stacy go with you to ask them? Your parents won't say *no* if they meet her.

Yeah! I'd love to meet your parents, Nicole.

Oh, OK.

B. What do you think will happen next? Explain.

6 If you need me, I'll be there.

Learning Goals

Communication
Describe personalities

Grammar
Adjectives and adverbs
If clauses to express future meaning

Vocabulary
Adjectives with negative prefixes

1 Reading

What kind of personality do you have? Take the quiz to find out. For each item, circle the letter next to your response.

PERSONALITY QUIZ

1. When you walk, you usually walk _____.
  a. quite fast, with long steps
  b. quite fast, with short, quick steps
  c. at an average speed, with your head up
  d. quite slowly, with your head down

2. When talking to people, you _____.
  a. fold your arms
  b. put your hands on your hips
  c. touch the person you are talking to
  d. play with your ear or smooth your hair

3. When relaxing on a sofa, you _____.
  a. put your legs neatly together
  b. cross your legs
  c. stretch out your legs
  d. curl one or both legs under you

4. When something really amuses you, you _____.
  a. laugh loudly
  b. laugh, but not too loudly
  c. chuckle quietly
  d. smile

5. When you go to a party, you _____.
  a. enter the room dramatically
  b. go straight to the most interesting-looking person in the room
  c. make a quiet entrance, looking around for someone you know
  d. make the quietest possible entrance

6. You are working hard. If someone interrupts you, you _____.
  a. welcome the break
  b. chat politely but hope the person will go away soon
  c. explain the situation and ask the person to come back later
  d. feel extremely irritated and look angry

7. Just before you go to sleep, you _____.
  a. lie on your back
  b. lie on your side, slightly curled
  c. lie on your stomach
  d. lie with your head under the covers

8. You often dream that you are _____.
  a. falling
  b. fighting or struggling
  c. searching for something or somebody
  d. flying or floating

See page 39 for scoring and rating your responses.

Your Score and Rating

To find out your score, give yourself four points for each a. response you circled, three points for each b. response you circled, two points for each c. response you circled, and one point for each d. response you circled. Then add up your points and read your rating below.

Over 28 points: People see you as exciting, unpredictable, and quick to make decisions. They admire you, but they don't always feel comfortable in your company.

20-27 points: People see you as lively, amusing, and interesting, and they enjoy your company. You enjoy being the center of attention, but you are not always sincere. You have a wide circle of friends.

12-19 points: People see you as sensible and practical but a little cautious. You do not make friends easily, but you are extremely loyal to the friends you make. You are always considerate, patient, and never unkind.

11 or under: People see you as shy, nervous, and indecisive. You work slowly and carefully. You often see problems that don't exist. You sometimes find it difficult to make new friends, but you are honest and always polite!

2 Vocabulary

Adjectives with negative prefixes

A. A prefix is one or more syllables added to the beginning of a word to change the word's meaning. Common prefixes that mean *not* are *dis-*, *in-*, *im-*, and *un-*.

Look at each pair of adjectives below. The second adjective in each pair has a negative prefix. Circle this prefix. Then, in your notebook, write the definitions of each word pair.

1. exciting—unexciting
   very interesting—not very interesting

2. loyal—disloyal
3. practical—impractical
4. decisive—indecisive

B. In your notebook, add the correct prefixes from Exercise A to the words below. Then write the meanings of the new words. Use a dictionary for help.

1. interesting
   uninteresting—not interesting

2. happy   5. honest
3. polite   6. sincere
4. comfortable   7. patient

3 Pronunciation

Word stress in adjectives

A. ⌒ Listen and repeat.

1. exciting—unexciting
2. loyal—disloyal
3. practical—impractical
4. decisive—indecisive

B. ⌒ Listen. Underline the syllable with the strongest stress in each word.

1. uninteresting
2. unhappy
3. polite
4. comfortable
5. honest
6. insincere
7. impatient

Adjectives and adverbs of manner

Adjectives	Adverbs	Examples
patient	patiently	Grace is **patient**. / She waited **patiently** for him.
careful	carefully	Ted is a **careful** driver. / He drives **carefully**.
easy	eas**ily**	This question is **easy**. / The class answered it **easily**.
fast	fast	Ken is a **fast** runner. / He runs **fast**.
hard	hard	They are **hard** workers. / They work **hard**.
early	early	I am an **early** riser. / I wake up **early**.
late	late	He is always **late**. / He wakes up **late**.
good	well	She is a **good** swimmer. / She swims **well**.

Remember! • An adjective describes a noun.

Ted is a **careful** driver.

• An adverb gives more information about a verb.

Ken runs **fast**.

• An adverb also gives more information about an adjective or another adverb.

Marcia is **very** strong.   Raul ran **too** slowly to win the race.

• Though many adverbs end in –*ly*, some do not. Therefore, use a dictionary when you are not sure of the form of an adverb.

4 Practice

Have a competition! Go to page 89.

5 Practice

Rewrite the sentences. Change the adjectives into adverbs.

1. Nicole has a soft voice.
   She speaks softly.

2. Chen is a hard worker.
   _____

3. Joan is a neat writer.
   _____

4. He's a good swimmer.
   _____

5. I am a careful driver.
   _____

6. You have a loud voice.
   _____

6 Communication

Describing personalities

🎧 **Listen. Then role-play the conversation with a partner.**

A: So, what kind of a person are you according to the Personality Quiz?

B: You won't believe it! It says I'm lively, amusing, and interesting. Do you agree?

A: Well, you're lively, but I'm not sure about amusing. Here's my rating. I'm exciting and unpredictable. And listen to this! People aren't always comfortable in my company. Is that true?

7 Your Turn

Work with two classmates. Discuss the results of your Personality Quiz. Are the results close to how people really see you?

8 Dialogue

🎧 **Listen and read.**

Nicole: Tom, thanks for understanding. It's not you; it's my parents.

Tom: It's OK. If there's any way I can help, you'll tell me, right?

Nicole: Absolutely!

Stacy: Boy, I'm glad that's all worked out. Do you guys want to hang out for a while at my house?

Tom: Sounds good to me. Nicole?

Nicole: Um, I'm going to have to pass.

Tom: Really? Are you sure you can't—even for an hour?

Nicole: No, really, I can't. If I don't get home soon, I won't have enough time to study.

Stacy: You mean, for the French test?

Nicole: Yes. If tomorrow's test is like the last one, I'm going to be in big trouble. I'll just catch the bus.

Tom: Oh, well. We can wait for the bus with you—right, Stacy?

Stacy: Oh, sure.

Nicole: You don't have to. Really.

Tom: Tell you what: If the bus doesn't come in 10 minutes, we'll just go.

Nicole: OK. It's a deal.

9 Comprehension

Discuss these questions as a class.

1. What does Nicole mean when she says, "It's not you; it's my parents."?
2. Why won't Nicole go to Stacy's house?
3. Was Nicole's last French test difficult or easy? How do you think Nicole did on the test?
4. How long will Stacy and Tom wait with Nicole for the bus?

If clauses to express future meaning

If I **need** your help, I**'ll tell** you.

If the test **is** difficult, I**'m going to be** in big trouble.

If the bus **doesn't come** in 10 minutes, we**'ll leave**.

If I **don't get** home soon, I **won't have** enough time to study.

Remember! • Use the present tense in the *if* clause. Use the future tense in the main clause.

• An *if* clause can come before or after a main clause.

If you need me, I'll be there.

I'll be there **if you need me**.

10 Practice

Read the cartoon. In your notebook, write what Sam is thinking. Use the cues.

1

Sam, are you going to call Kristi today to ask her to the prom?

I don't know, Mom.

(1)
If Kristi says no, I'll feel awful.
(Kristi say no / feel awful)

2

Come on, Sam! She's such a nice girl.

I know, Mom.

(2) _____
(you keep asking me about it / never call her)

3

Here's the phone. Why don't you call her?

No, Mom! Not right now!

(3) _____
(call Kristi / need privacy!)

4

OK, then. I guess I should take Buster out.

OK, Mom.

(4) _____
(she go out / call Kristi)

5

I'll get it.

(5) _____
(not Kristi / be really disappointed)

Is that for me, Mom?

Yes, it's Kristi.

(6) _____
(get the courage / ask her to the prom)

6

Hi, Sam. Do you have a date for the prom yet? Do you want to go with me?

Well, . . . er . . . um. . . uh . . .

7

I'll ask Ted instead.

Forget it! Bye.

Oh, no! What did I just do?

RRRRING

Progress Check *Units 5 and 6*

Grammar

A. Fill in the blanks with the adjective or adverb form of the word in italics. (1 point each)

1. *quick*
   a. Would you like to have a ___quick___ lunch?
   b. We ate lunch ___quickly___ because we were late for the party.

2. *early*
   a. The employees left work _____.
   b. My family usually has an _____ dinner on weekdays.

3. *careful*
   a. Molly works _____ on all her assignments.
   b. She is such a _____ worker.

4. *fluent*
   a. Yon Mi is _____ in English.
   b. She speaks English _____.

5. *heavy*
   a. Why does she walk so _____?
   b. This table is too _____ for us to move.

B. Combine each pair of sentences into one sentence by using an *if* clause. (2 points each)

1. Maybe Dad won't be tired tonight. He'll go to the gym.
   If Dad is not tired tonight, he'll go to the gym.

2. Maybe she'll come home early today. We'll go jogging.
   _____

3. Maybe Stanley will be in a good mood. Lucy will ask him to go shopping with her.
   _____

4. Maybe you'll write him. He'll write you back.
   _____

5. Maybe he'll call tonight. I won't be upset with him.
   _____

6. Maybe Bruce will come to visit. We'll watch a video together.
   _____

Vocabulary

C. Match an adjective from the box with the correct definition. (2 points each)

honest	indecisive	practical
loyal	impatient	polite

___indecisive___ 1. A person who cannot make up his or her mind.

_____ 2. A person who is courteous and well mannered.

_____ 3. A person who is realistic and reasonable.

_____ 4. A person who is truthful.

_____ 5. A person who is faithful and true.

_____ 6. A person who is restless and short tempered.

Communication

D. Work with a partner. In your notebook, write a conversation describing your ideal friend or ideal person. Use adjectives and adverbs in your conversation. (5 points)

A: What's your idea of an ideal friend?
B: An ideal friend? Let me see. My ideal friend is honest. She is also very loyal.

Wide Angle on the world

1 Reading

A. Read the article about the '70s.

B. Answer the questions about the article.

1. List at least three examples of technological change in the '70s.

   _____

2. What did women wear more often in the '70s?

   _____

3. Why was the '70s video game named "Pong"?

   _____

4. What food did the astronauts bring into space?

   _____

5. What social change of the '60s was evident in the TV series *Charlie's Angels*?

   _____

2 Listening

A. 🎧 **Listen to a dance instructor explain how to do the Bump. Then listen again and fill in the blanks.**

B. With a partner, stand up, follow the directions, and practice the Bump.

Do the Bump

1. Bend _____ slightly.
2. Move your weight from _____ to the _____.
3. Keep your _____ bent at the _____.
4. You can _____ your partner's elbows, _____, or feet.
5. You have to _____ and almost _____ when you bump.
6. You can _____ your hands _____ your head when you bump.
7. You always have to bump exactly _____.

3 Writing and Speaking

Work with a partner. Use the categories below to talk about and list new trends and tastes in this decade. Then discuss your list with another group.

Fashion   Games/Entertainment
Music   Dance
Food   TV shows

PONG

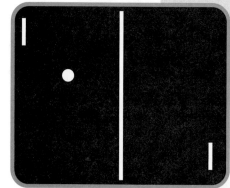

THE '70s

The '70s were a time of social and technological change. Astronauts flew to the moon, women fought for their equal rights, and life was lived a little bit faster and looser. As a result, new trends and tastes in fashion, recreation, entertainment, food, and TV shows sprang up[1].

In fashion, clothes were suddenly more casual. Men unbuttoned the top two, three, or even four buttons on their shirts to reveal gold chains around their necks. Women wore pants more often—from hip-hugger blue jeans at home to pants suits with boots at work. Hair was longer on both men and women, and everyone had a blow-dryer.

People went out more. Disco dancing in clubs—to music by the Bee Gees, Donna Summer, and the Village People—was very popular. Disco music was easy to dance to. It had a heavy one-two bass beat sweetened[2] by horns and a new instrument, the synthesizer. Cool dance steps included the Hustle, the Bump, and the Bus Stop.

New technology brought new entertainment and even new foods. The first successful video game was released in 1971: "Pong." Pong was a black-and-white screen with the image of a ping-pong table. The screen was placed in the middle of a wooden table, and players paid a quarter to hit the ball back and forth.

The astronauts who flew to the moon took food with them on their trips, and this food was a hit[3] back home. Space Food Sticks were like candy bars—soft, sweet, chewy food sticks inside cool foil pouches. Popular flavors were chocolate, caramel, and peanut butter.

TV shows reflected some of the social changes of the '60s. While women were getting equal rights and moving into jobs only men used to have, a new show called *Charlie's Angels* became a big hit. The show was about three beautiful female agents who always captured the bad guys by the end of the show. Their boss, however, was still a man.

Each decade offers new technology, new social changes, with new trends and tastes. What's your decade like?

1. **sprang up:** came into being
2. **sweetened:** made pleasant
3. **a hit:** a popular food, show, etc.

7 Have you seen his new jeans?

Learning Goals

Communication
Offer, refuse, and accept help

Grammar
The present perfect for the indefinite past
The present perfect with *for* and *since*

Vocabulary
Clothes and personal possessions

1 Dialogue

🎧 **Listen and read.**

Stacy: Hey, Justin! Check these out. These tops are wild!

Justin: Wow! Cool! So, Stacy, have you seen Ben's new jeans? Well, they're not really new! Straight out of the 60s, I think.

Stacy: What, like big bell bottoms?

Justin: Uh-huh. And patches and stuff.

Clerk: Hi. Do you need any help?

Stacy: No, thanks. We're just looking.

Justin: Have you ever been to that new vintage clothing store . . . something Rose?

Stacy: Oh, you mean "Second Hand Rose"?

Justin: Yeah, that's it.

Stacy: Uh-huh. I've been in there a couple of times, but just to look. I've never actually bought vintage clothing. It's not my thing.

Justin: I can relate to that!

2 Comprehension

Discuss these questions as a class.

1. What do Stacy and Justin think of the tops?
2. What do Ben's jeans look like?
3. What kind of clothes do they sell at Second Hand Rose?
4. Has Stacy ever bought any clothes at Second Hand Rose? Why?

3 Useful Phrases

🎧 **Listen and repeat.**

- Check these out.
- Straight out of the 60s.
- It's not my thing.
- I can relate to that!

4 Vocabulary

Clothes and personal possessions

Circle the item that does <u>not</u> belong in the group.

1. wallet   purse   briefcase   (top)
2. shoes   socks   jacket   slippers
3. watch   belt   necklace   earrings
4. coat   jeans   pants   shorts
5. skirt   sneakers   sweater   dress

5 Communication

Offering and refusing or accepting help

🎧 **Listen and read. Then role-play the conversations.**

A: Do you need any help?
B: No, thanks. We're just looking.

A: Do you need any help?
B: Yes, please. Do you have this in red?
A: I'm sure we do. What size?
B: Medium, please.
A: Here you go.
B: Thanks. Can I try it on?
A: Yes. The fitting room is straight ahead to your right.
B: Thanks.

6 Your Turn

Work with two classmates. Answer these questions.

1. a. Do you shop for your own clothes? If not, who buys your
      clothes for you?
   b. Do you like the clothes this person chooses for you? Why or
      why not?
2. Have you ever bought vintage clothing? Why or why not?

GRAMMAR FOCUS

The present perfect for the indefinite past

Affirmative statements
I **have** (I**'ve**) **been** in there a couple of times.
He **has** (He**'s**) **shopped** there once or twice.

Yes/No **questions**
Have you **seen** Ben's jeans?
Has she **ever bought** anything there?

Negative statements
I **have not** (**haven't**) **seen** her new clothes.
She **has never worn** vintage clothing.

Short answers
Yes, I **have**. / No, I **haven't**.
Yes, she **has**. / No, she **hasn't**.

Remember! • Use *have* or *has* and the past participle to form the present perfect.
• Use the present perfect to talk about things that happened at some indefinite time in the past.
• You can use *ever* with the present perfect in questions.
• You can use *never* with the present perfect in negative answers.

7 Practice

Have a competition! Go to page 89.

8 Pronunciation

The sounds /b/ and /v/

A. ∩ Listen and read.

/b/	/v/
been	very
bought	never
bell	they've

B. Work with a partner. Read the dialogues aloud. Switch roles.

A: Have you ever worn bell bottoms?
B: No, I haven't.

A: Have they ever bought vintage clothing?
B: Yes, they have.

9 Practice

Fill in the blanks with the present perfect tense of the verbs in parentheses. You may use contractions.

1. She *(buy)* **'s bought** a lot of things there.
2. He *(never / see)* _____ them before.
3. We *(shop)* _____ there once or twice.
4. Linda *(never / meet)* _____ Ken.
5. They *(go)* _____ out a few times.
6. She *(not / call)* _____ her mother in a long time.
7. I *(never / be)* _____ to Brazil.
8. He *(watch)* _____ that TV show a few times.

10 Practice

Work with a partner. In your notebook, write *Yes/No* questions for each of the sentences in Exercise 9. Then write short answers, using the information.

Example:

Has she bought a lot of things there?

Yes, she has.

The present perfect with *for* **and** *since*

for	*since*
The store has been open **for** two months.	The store has been open **since** May.
I've known him **for** about three years.	I've known him **since** January 2002.
Information questions	**Short answers**
	For a few years.
How long have you worked there?	**Since** 2002.

Remember! • Use *for* and a length of time to say how long a situation has lasted.
• Use *since* and a point in time to say when something began.
• Use *how long* with the present perfect for questions.

11 Practice

Complete the magazine article about Jennifer Lopez. Fill in the blanks with the present perfect tense of the verb in parentheses or choose between *for* and *since*. Write your answers in the blanks.

J.LO–Jennifer Lopez *(1. be)* __has been__ in show business *(2. for / since)* __since__ 1990, when she started out as a dancer on the TV show, "In Living Color." Her big break came in 1997 with the bio-movie *Selena*. *(3. For / Since)* _____ that year, Lopez *(4. appear)* _____ in several big movie hits, including *The Cell* and *Maid in Manhattan*.

Lopez is also a successful singer. Her album, *On the 6*, *(5. sell)* _____ almost 2.8 million copies *(6. for / since)* _____ 1999, when it first came out. J.Lo continues to record albums and make music videos even though she's busy with her movie career.

Lopez's sense of style *(7. attract)* _____ a lot of attention *(8. for / since)* _____ her big break in 1997. So it was no surprise when, in 2001, she started her own clothing line and perfume label, J.Lo. The clothes she designs *(9. be)* _____ in stores *(10. for / since)* _____ less than two years, but people love them. Her clothes are a hit in a very tough industry.

12 Reading

Read the article below. As you read, think about some clothes and accessories you have worn. What were they? What did your parents think of them?

The Mystery of Teen Fashion

Teen fashion is intriguing and fascinating. We've all noticed teens with neon-colored hair, pierced tongues, and bare stomachs. We've seen teenagers use common household items like safety pins and rubber bands as accessories. So, where do these trends come from? Who starts them? And who dictates to the world's teen population when something suddenly becomes cool?

Consulting companies that specialize in the youth market track down teen trends to find out what the next "must-haves" will be. One of these companies is *Lambesis*, whose trend spotters travel all over the world, read hundreds of magazines, and watch thousands of hours of movies and television in their quest for what is cool. The parks and streets of big U.S. cities and the campuses of small-town colleges have become their hunting grounds. According to one expert on youth culture, many trends simply boil down to "whatever's cheap and whatever will shock people." Teens often compete to see who can be the most cutting-edge, and fashion is no exception. They find ways to wear everyday accessories in a new and different style. One student started wearing her watch on her ankle. "She could never really read the watch," another student said. "It was just more to make a statement."

Although teens themselves have often been trend starters, the biggest influence on teen fashion, of course, has always been pop culture. TV shows, music, movies, magazines, and celebrities have had a huge impact on teen style. Many teenagers choose to dress like popular teen singing sensations.

The size of the teen market has grown steadily. Today, it is estimated to be a staggering $100 billion a year. No wonder clothing companies spend millions of dollars trying to identify the next hot teen trend!

13 Comprehension

Answer the following questions.

1. What fashion trends are mentioned in the first paragraph?
2. What do trend spotters do to find out about the latest hot thing in teen fashion?
3. What is the biggest influence on teen fashion?
4. Why do clothing companies spend millions of dollars to research teen fashion trends?

14 Speaking

Do a class survey. In your notebook, make a chart like the one below. Interview six students in your class. Put the girls' and boys' answers in different columns.

	Girls	Boys
What influences you when you buy clothes?		

15 Writing

Write a summary of the results of your survey. In general, what influences girls when they buy clothes? What influences boys?

At the Pet Store

🎧 Read the story and write the missing sentences. Choose from the sentences in the box. Then listen and check your work.

You know, my grades haven't been that good this year. He's had it for five years now.
And my grades have started to get better. So, has everything worked out OK
Have you ever had a pet? between you and your parents?

1.
Hi, Tom. How did you find me?
Justin told me about your new job.

2.
This is my uncle's pet store.
(1) _____
I'm glad your parents let you take a job.

3.
(2)_____
Yeah. My dad said that I overreacted to his rules.

4.
(3)_____
I know. But you're studying harder now, right?

5.
Oh, yeah.
(4) _____
That's great. . . . This is a cute dog. But I like cats better.

6.
OK, here's a cat for you. Meet Agent.
(5) _____
No, never, but maybe Agent should be my first!

8

He's the one who gave him a D.

Learning Goals

Communication
Talk about school experiences

Grammar
The present perfect with *yet* and *already*

The present perfect contrasted with the simple past

Adjective clauses with *who*, *that*, and *where*

Vocabulary
Expressions related to school

1 Dialogue

🎧 **Listen and read.**

Tom: So, Stacy, have you asked your parents about the Sea World trip yet?

Stacy: Yeah, I asked them yesterday. They won't let me go!

Steve: Bummer! How come?

Stacy: I have to do a book report for English, and I haven't read the book yet!

Tom: Too bad. Who do you have for English?

Stacy: Mr. Arnold. He's the one who gave James a D last year.

Tom: Oh, yeah. I've heard about Mr. Arnold. I hope I never get him.

Steve: The class that I'm really worried about is economics. It's hard!

Stacy: Have you had any tests yet?

Steve: Yes, we've already had three. I did OK on them, but I had to study a lot.

Tom: It's so hard for me to study at home. It's always really noisy at my house and I can't concentrate.

Stacy: Hey, Tom, I know this great place where it's totally quiet and no one bothers you.

Tom: Really?

Stacy: Yeah. It's called the library!

2 Comprehension

Discuss these questions as a class.

1. Why can't Stacy go to Sea World?
2. How do the kids feel about Mr. Arnold?
3. Which class is Steve worried about? Why?
4. Why does Tom have trouble studying?

3 Useful Phrases

A. 🎧 **Listen and repeat.**

- Bummer!
- How come?
- Too bad.

B. Work with a partner. Write a dialogue using the phrases in Exercise A. Then role-play the conversation.

4 Vocabulary

Expressions related to school

Look at the sentences in Column A. Match them with the sentences in Column B that have the same meaning. Write the letters.

	A	**B**
_d_ 1.	I hope I get Ms. Barr next year.	a. My grade on the test was pretty good.
___ 2.	Who do you have for English?	b. James almost failed the class.
___ 3.	That teacher gave James a D.	c. Who's your English teacher?
___ 4.	I did OK on the test.	d. I hope Ms. Barr will be my teacher next year.

The present perfect with *yet* and *already*

Affirmative statements with *already*
We**'ve already had** the test.
I**'ve already read** the book.

Yes/No* questions with *yet
Has she **asked** her parents about the trip **yet**?
Have you **had** any tests **yet**?

Negative statements with *yet*
We **haven't had** the test **yet**.
I **haven't read** the book **yet**.

Short answers
Yes, she **has**. / No, she **hasn't**.
Yes, I **have**. / No, I **haven't**.

5 Practice

Steve is planning a trip to Sea World. Stacy is planning how to do her book report.
Look at their "To Do" lists. They've put check marks next to the things they've
already done. In your notebook, write a sentence about each item on their lists.

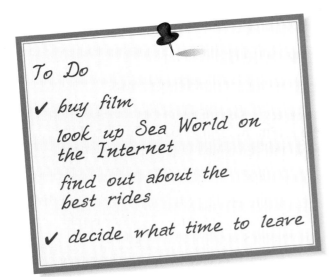

To Do
✔ buy film
look up Sea World on the Internet
find out about the best rides
✔ decide what time to leave

To Do
✔ ask Mr. Arnold for more time
read the book!
✔ talk to Justin about the report
write the report

Examples:

1. *Steve has already bought film.*

2. *Steve hasn't looked up Sea World on the Internet yet.*

The present perfect contrasted with the simple past

The present perfect
I**'ve read** that book already.
She**'s been** to Sea World several times.
We **haven't seen** the movie yet.

The simple past
You **read** that book last week.
He **went** to Sea World last year.
They **didn't see** the movie last night.

Remember! Use the present perfect for activities that happened at an indefinite time in the past.
Use the simple past for activities that were completed at a specific time in the past.

6 Practice

Read the descriptions of Mr. Arnold. First, write sentences using the simple past in your notebook. Then write sentences using the present perfect.

When he first became a teacher:	For the last few years:
1. he / not be / demanding or strict *He was not demanding or strict.*	1. he / be demanding and strict *He's been demanding and strict.*
2. everyone / pass / his class	2. some of his students / get bad grades
3. no one / work hard	3. everyone / have to work hard
4. his students / not learn much	4. his students / learn a lot

7 Communication

Talking about school experiences

A. ⌒ Listen and read.

Nicole: Have you gotten back your report from Mr. Arnold yet?

Justin: Yeah. I got an A.

Nicole: Wow! That's great. What's Mr. Arnold like?

Justin: He's really strict. He's the toughest teacher I've ever had. His class is really demanding!

B. Work with a partner. Write a similar dialogue in your notebook. Then role-play the dialogue.

GRAMMAR FOCUS

Adjective clauses with *who*, *that*, and *where*

Mr. Arnold was the teacher **who gave James a D**.
The boy **that she's going out with** is my neighbor.
I love the outfit **that you wore to the party last night**!
The gym **where she goes** is expensive.

Remember! • An adjective clause has a subject and a verb. It describes or gives more information about a noun. It comes after the noun it describes. It cannot stand alone as a sentence.
• *Who* refers to people; *where* refers to places; *that* can refer to people, places, or things.

8 Practice

Read the dialogue on page 52 again. Underline the adjective clauses.

9 Practice

Combine each pair of sentences into one by using either *who*, *that*, or *where*. Make the *b* sentences the adjective clauses.

1. a. I have a neighbor.
   b. The neighbor is very quiet and shy.
   I have a neighbor who is very quiet and shy.

2. a. That's the restaurant.
   b. I met him for the first time.
   _____

3. a. We need another person.
   b. The person can help us finish this project.
   _____

4. a. Brad Pitt was in the same hotel.
   b. We stayed in the hotel.
   _____

5. a. Do you like the car?
   b. Your parents bought the car.
   _____

Unit 8   55

10 Reading

Read the article below about different groups of teens. Do you know anyone who belongs in each group?

Teen World

Like many other groups, teenagers can be classified into different sub-groups. These are based on attitude, appearance, and lifestyle. Here are a few sub-groups for 21st Century teens.

Edge Teens

We have seen them around, and for sure, we have raised our eyebrows at the way they look. They are Edge Teens. Edge Teens are teenagers who are on the cutting edge of teenage fashion and lifestyle. And yet they are often anti-fashion and anti-style. They are usually very smart, but they are not often the best students. Edge Teens do not worry about the future; they want to have fun NOW! They like dance and rave, techno and punk, but not rap, hip-hop, or R&B. They are teens who have their bodies pierced and wear day-glo hair.

Influencers

Influencers are always popular and influential. How do they differ from Edge Teens? Influencers are more "mainstream cool." They are teenagers who care about how they look and what they wear. They are outgoing and confident. They like having boyfriends and girlfriends, using cell phones, participating in sports, and hanging out at malls. They wear the latest fashion, and they watch music videos and movies more than other teens. These are the teenagers whom most other teenagers "wanna be like."

Conformers

About 50 percent of the teen population belongs in this group. They are typical teens, who conform to the latest teen behaviors, styles, and trends. Sometimes they try to be like Influencers; sometimes like Edge Teens. They follow the lifestyles and fashion already adopted by others. Conformers like to follow trends rather than set them.

11 Comprehension

In your own words, describe the sub-groups below. Discuss them as a class.

- Edge Teens
- Influencers
- Conformers

12 Your Turn

In a small group, just for fun, discuss this question: Which teen group would you like to belong to? Why?

13 Writing

What is your opinion about categorizing people? In your notebook, write a paragraph expressing your opinion. In the first sentence, give your opinion. In the other sentences, support your opinion with details, such as facts and examples.

Progress Check *Units 7 and 8*

Grammar

A. Write sentences using the present perfect tense. Use the cues. Use contractions when possible. (2 points each)

1. My brother/lose the house keys several times this week

   My brother has lost the house keys several

   times this week.

2. I/never be/to a costume party

   _____

3. We/never try/sushi

   _____

4. They/know/each other for 50 years

   _____

5. Julie/never go/camping

   _____

6. She/always like/that TV show

   _____

B. Fill in the blanks with either the simple past or the present perfect tense. Use contractions when possible. (1 point each)

1. *(eat)*

   A: *Have* you ever *eaten* in a French restaurant?

   B: Yes, I _____ at Pierre's last night.

2. *(live)*

   A: What cities _____ you _____ in?

   B: I _____ in Chicago, San Francisco, and New York.

3. *(see)*

   A: _____ you guys _____ the new Harry Potter movie yet?

   B: Yes. We _____ already _____ it twice.

4. *(be)*

   A: _____ they _____ to the mall yet?

   B: Yes. They _____ there last weekend.

Vocabulary

C. Read the 12 clothing words in the box. Circle them in the puzzle. (2 points each)

belt	briefcase	coat	dress
jacket	jeans	pants	shoes
slippers	socks	top	watch

```
J  B  C  E  I  L  O  P  R  W
A  E  O  D  D  R  E  S  S  A
C  T  A  B  F  L  T  G  L  T
K  F  T  N  E  R  M  O  I  C
E  A  P  H  S  L  N  K  P  H
T  S  Q  U  I  F  T  M  P  Y
M  A  H  P  A  N  T  S  E  J
B  S  G  O  R  H  T  Y  R  W
V  B  R  I  E  F  C  A  S  E
W  N  U  B  L  S  O  C  K  S
```

Communication

D. Work with a partner. A is a salesperson at a department store. She is asking B if she needs help. B is a customer looking for a dress for her prom. Complete the conversation. (5 points)

A: _____?

B: Yes, please. I'm looking for a dress for my prom. _____?

A: Yes, we do. What color and size?

B: _____, please.

A: Here are a few. Would you like to try them on?

B: Yes, please. _____?

A: The fitting room is straight ahead and to the right.

SONG

Lifehouse

Lifehouse lead singer Jason Wade began singing and writing songs when he was 12. When he was 15, he moved to Los Angeles and met Guatamala-born Sergio Andrade. They formed a band and began playing together on Friday nights. They were later discovered by Dreamworks Records, and their first album featured the smash hit "Hanging by a Moment."

Hanging by a Moment

Chorus

Desperate for changing
Starving for truth
I'm closer to where I started
I'm chasing after you
I'm (1.) __falling__ even more in love with you
Letting go of all I've held onto
I'm (2.) _____ here until you make me move
I'm hanging by a moment here with you

Forgetting all I'm lacking
Completely incomplete
I'll take your invitation
You take all of me

Now I'm (3.) _____ even more in love with you
Letting go of all I've held on to
I'm (4.) _____ here until you make me move
I'm hanging by a moment here with you

I'm living for the only thing I know
I'm (5.) _____ and not quite sure where to go
And I don't know what I'm diving into
Just hanging by a moment here with you

There is nothing else to lose
There is nothing else to find
There is (6.) _____ in the world that could change my mind
There is (7.) _____ else

Repeat line three times

Repeat chorus

I'm living for the only thing I know
I'm (8.) _____ and not quite sure where to go
And I don't know what I'm diving into
Just hanging by a moment here with you

Repeat line five times

1. 🎧 **Listen to the song and fill in the blanks with the words below. (Each word appears two times.)**

running	standing	falling	nothing

2. **How does the singer feel about the person he's singing to? Why do you think so?**

3. **Think of a time when you thought, "There is nothing in the world that could change my mind." Tell a classmate about it.**

GAME Stomp, Spin, and Spell

Steps

1. Play this game standing in small groups.

2. One student is the "spellmaster" and can keep his or her book open. The other students close their books.

3. The spellmaster says a word from the list and then asks a student to spell it. The student spells the word aloud, but uses actions instead of letters for *s*,

t, *e*, and *i*. If the student spells and "acts" the word correctly, he or she gets a point.

4. If the student does not spell it and act it out correctly, the spellmaster spells it and acts it out. The spellmaster then gives the next student a word.

5. The student with the most points at the end of the game wins.

s= stomp

t= spin

e= clap

i= hop

impolite	strict	promise
tolerant	assignment	unexciting
vegetable	indecisive	attended
patiently	starving	disappointed
briefcase	message	slippers
discussing	straight	independent

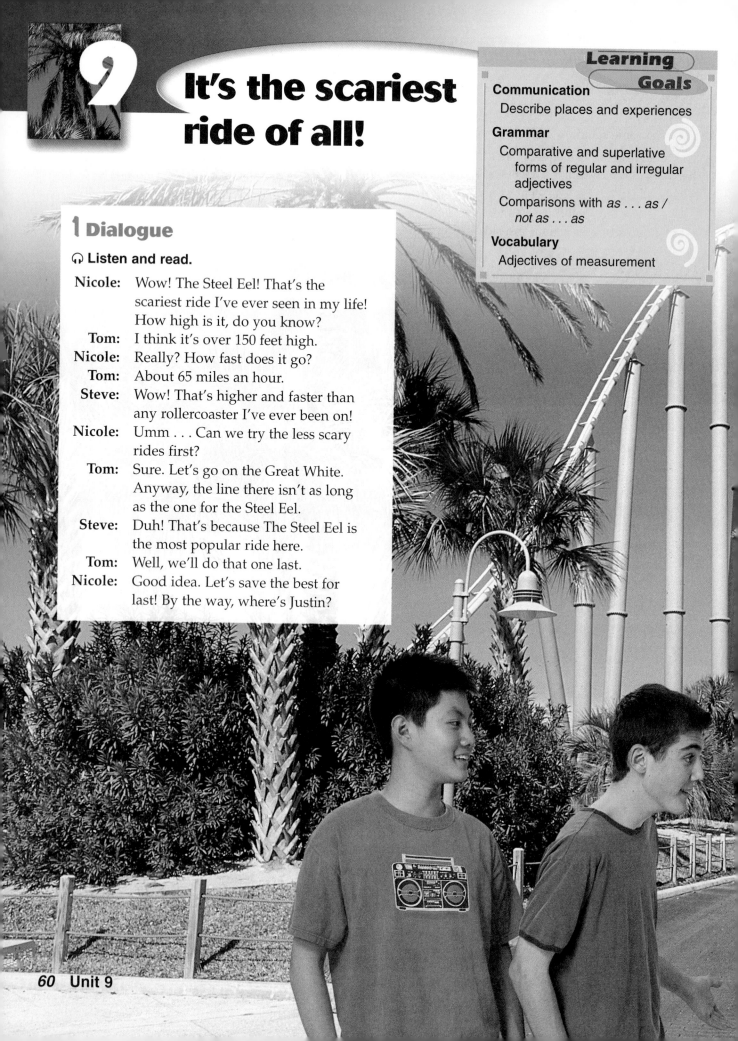

9

It's the scariest ride of all!

Learning Goals

Communication
Describe places and experiences

Grammar
Comparative and superlative forms of regular and irregular adjectives

Comparisons with *as . . . as / not as . . . as*

Vocabulary
Adjectives of measurement

1 Dialogue

🎧 **Listen and read.**

Nicole: Wow! The Steel Eel! That's the scariest ride I've ever seen in my life! How high is it, do you know?

Tom: I think it's over 150 feet high.

Nicole: Really? How fast does it go?

Tom: About 65 miles an hour.

Steve: Wow! That's higher and faster than any rollercoaster I've ever been on!

Nicole: Umm . . . Can we try the less scary rides first?

Tom: Sure. Let's go on the Great White. Anyway, the line there isn't as long as the one for the Steel Eel.

Steve: Duh! That's because The Steel Eel is the most popular ride here.

Tom: Well, we'll do that one last.

Nicole: Good idea. Let's save the best for last! By the way, where's Justin?

2 Comprehension

Discuss these questions as a class.

1. Where do you think the three friends are?
2. How does Nicole feel about riding The Steel Eel?
3. What's Tom's advice about deciding which ride to go on first?

3 Useful Phrases

A. 🎧 Listen and repeat.

- Duh!
- Let's save the best for last.
- By the way, . . .

B. Work with a partner. Choose one of the phrases and write a short conversation. Then role-play the conversation.

4 Vocabulary

Adjectives of measurement

Write the adjectives in the box under the correct category. *Long* and *short* each belong in two categories.

- fast—slow
- high—low
- long—short
- heavy—light

Height	Weight	Length	Duration	Speed
high	___	___	___	___
___	___	___	___	___

5 Communication

Describing places and experiences

A. 🎧 Listen to the conversation.

A: Did you go on the Great White?
B: Absolutely! It was really scary!
A: How fast does it go?
B: About 50 miles an hour.
A: Really? How long is it?
B: It's 2,500 feet long.
A: Cool! I'll try it later.

B. Write a similar conversation about Medusa, a roller coaster at Six Flags in New Jersey. Use the phrases below and the information in the chart on page 62.

How high . . .	How fast . . .
How long . . .	

GRAMMAR FOCUS

Comparative and superlative forms of regular adjectives

Positive	Comparative	Superlative
clean	clean**er** than	the clean**est**
hot	hot**ter** than	the hot**test**
happy	happ**ier** than	the happ**iest**
famous	**more** famous than	the **most** famous

Comparative and superlative forms of irregular adjectives

Positive	Comparative	Superlative
good	**better** than	the **best**
bad	**worse** than	the **worst**
far	**farther** than	the **farthest**

Remember! • Use the comparative to compare two people, places, and things.
- Use the superlative to compare one person, place, or thing to two or more other people, places, and things.
- You can also use *less than* or *the least* to compare things.
  The amusement park is **less popular than** the beach.
  That book is **the least exciting** of all the books she wrote.
- *Less* means the opposite of *more. Least* means the opposite of *most.*

6 Practice

Have a competition! Go to page 90.

7 Practice

Read the information in the chart below about three of the rides at Six Flags in New Jersey. In your notebook, write three sentences for each adjective below, comparing the three rides. First write a sentence with the positive form of the adjective. Use the comparative form in your second sentence and the superlative form in your third sentence. You may also use *less than / least.*

high	long	fast	short

	Nitro	Medusa	Batman & Robin
Height	230 feet (23 stories)	142 feet (about 14 stories)	200 feet (20 stories)
Length	5,394 feet (1+ miles)	3,985 feet	2,366 feet (Batman: 1,137 ft.; Robin: 1,229 ft.)
Top speed	80 mph	61 mph	70 mph
Ride duration	4 minutes	3 minutes, 15 seconds	45 seconds

1. high
   a. *Medusa is high.*
   b. *Batman & Robin is higher than Medusa.*
   c. *Nitro is the highest of the three rides.*

8 Practice

In your notebook, write sentences comparing the items listed below. Use the positive, comparative, and superlative forms of the irregular adjectives in parentheses.

1. three TV programs (*good*)
   a. *Gilmore Girls is a good show.*
   b. *Friends is better than Gilmore Girls.*
   c. *Alias is the best of the three shows.*

2. three movies (*bad*)

3. three singers (*good*)

4. distance of three other countries from your country (*far*)

GRAMMAR FOCUS

Making comparisons with *as . . . as* / *not as . . . as*

The beach is **as popular as** the amusement park.
The book is **not as exciting as** the movie.

Remember! • Use *as + adjective + as* to say that there is no difference between two people or things.
• Use *not as + adjective + as* to say that there is a difference between two people or things.

9 Practice

Look at the graph below. Then, in your notebook, write sentences comparing the popularity of the free-time activities. Use the word *popular* and the cues.

1. (*the most*) *Television is the most popular.*
2. (*the least*)
3. (*as . . . as*)
4. (*not as . . . as*)
5. (*less . . . than*)

10 Listening

⌾ **Listen to the conversation. Then write *T* for each true statement and *F* for each false statement.**

_T_ 1. Stacy did not go on The Steel Eel.

_____ 2. Nicole enjoyed riding on The Steel Eel.

_____ 3. Steve was really scared while riding on The Steel Eel.

_____ 4. Tom had an embarrassing experience at the mall.

_____ 5. Steve thinks that Justin's story is funny.

_____ 6. Nicole wants to hear about the adventure at the mall.

11 Reading

Read about the awesome power and speed of Superman the Escape.

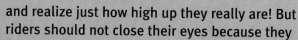

SUPERMAN THE ESCAPE

Faster than a speeding bullet . . . more powerful than a locomotive . . . Superman the Escape at Six Flags Magic Mountain in Valencia, California is the world's tallest and fastest roller coaster. It's an unbelievable 40 stories high and 900 feet long.

Each Superman train seats fifteen riders. The front and second rows are the best seats for people who want to enjoy the view. Riders are held inside the cars by nothing more than a lap bar. Superman takes only seven seconds to reach its maximum flight speed of 100 miles per hour.

As the trains shoot up into the sky, riders are often amazed—or scared—when they look down

and realize just how high up they really are! But riders should not close their eyes because they might miss Superman himself, looking down at them from the top of the tower. That's a sight which is almost as thrilling as the ride.

Then, after a brief stop at the top, the cars change directions and free fall backwards. Riders experience weightlessness for six and a half seconds before they speed up to 100 miles per hour again. Just before the cars reenter the launch chamber, the magnetic braking system kicks in, and the cars slow down to a reasonable speed. The entire experience takes just 23 seconds!

12 Comprehension

Discuss the question below as a class.

What features and actions make Superman the Escape scarier and more thrilling than other roller coasters?

13 Your Turn

Work with a small group. Talk about the most exciting—or the most unforgettable experience—you have ever had. Include the following information:

1. where you went
2. when you went there
3. who you were with
4. what you did there
5. what the most exciting (or the most unforgettable) thing was and why

14 Writing

Write a short paragraph about the experience you shared in Exercise 13. Illustrate your paragraph with drawings or photographs. Then post your paragraph on the class bulletin board.

Learn to Learn

Reading maps in brochures and guides

When you visit a theme park or another tourist attraction, always pick up a brochure and guide. The maps inside them will have valuable information, such as a compass, your location, the main sites of interest, restaurants, and transportation. Using simple maps like these can enhance your map-reading skills and improve your English vocabulary.

The Day After Sea World

10 I was running when I fell.

Learning Goals

Communication
Talk about a past incident

Grammar
The past continuous: statements and information questions

Vocabulary
Action verbs

1 Vocabulary

Action verbs

Look at the picture. Label the actions with the verbs in the box.

bounced	cut
broke	fainted
burned	fell
crashed	kicked
crossed	sprained

1. *fell*

2.

3.

4.

2 Pronunciation

Words beginning with *r-* blends

A. 🎧 **Listen and repeat.**

break	drop
bread	group
crash	praise
cross	trash

B. 🎧 **Listen and repeat. Circle the words beginning with *r-* blends.**

1. Don't (drop) the (bread) on the floor.
2. Did my sister grab the crayon?
3. The van crashed into a trash can.
4. Claire broke her promise to her friend.
5. Try to stay with the group.

3 Communication

Talking about a past incident

🎧 **Listen. Then role-play the conversation.**

A: What happened? I heard somebody cry for help.
B: There was an accident over there.
A: Was it bad?
B: Two cars crashed, a biker broke his leg, and somebody else fainted. But no one was seriously hurt.
A: Thank goodness.
B: And all that because a duck and her babies were trying to cross the street!

4 Dialogue

🎧 **Listen and read.**

Josh: Oops! Watch out! . . . I'm really sorry. Are you all right?

Stacy: I don't think so. My right ankle hurts. Ouch!

Josh: My ankle hurts, too. I think I've sprained it.

Nicole: Stacy! Are you OK?

Tom: Should I call 911?

Stacy: No, don't. Let me just sit here for a minute.

Josh: It was my fault. I was going really fast when I crashed into you.

Stacy: It's OK. I wasn't paying attention. You suddenly appeared while I was looking the other way.

Justin: All right, you guys. Let's get the two of you to a hospital—just to make sure you're OK.

Josh: My car is parked across the street. Can one of you drive?

Tom: I can.

Justin: Let's go then. Nicole, help me with Stacy, please.

Tom: And I'll walk him to the car. By the way, what's your name?

Josh: Josh. Josh Grant.

5 Comprehension

Read the sentences. Then write the correct responses.

1. They were both hurt in the rollerblading accident. ___Josh___ and _____

2. He wants to call 911. _____

3. He has a car. _____

4. He will drive everyone to the hospital. _____

5. In the United States, you call this number whenever there is an emergency. _____

6 Useful Phrases

🎧 **Listen and read. Then role-play the conversation.**

A: Watch out! Are you all right?
B: I don't think so.
A: Should I call 911?
B: No, don't. Let me just sit here for a minute.

GRAMMAR FOCUS

The past continuous: statements

Bruce **was watching** TV at ten o'clock last night.
While Bruce **was watching** TV, his cell phone rang.
Josh **was going** really fast *when* he crashed into Stacy.
While Josh **was rollerblading** in the park, his brother **was playing** video games.

Remember! • The past continuous describes an activity that was in progress at a particular time in the past.
• Often, the **past continuous** is used with the *while* clause; the **simple past** is often used with the *when* clause.
• When two actions are in progress at the same time, use the **past continuous** for both clauses.

7 Practice

In your notebook, combine the sentences. Use the past continuous, the simple past, and the cues.

1. I *(wait)* for the light to turn green. Shakira *(walk)* by. *(While)*
   While I was waiting for the light to turn green, Shakira walked by.
2. We *(rollerblade)* at the park. The accident *(happen)*. *(When)*
3. The mayor *(deliver)* his speech. Several cell phones *(ring)*. *(While)*
4. Uncle Bill *(watch)* Friends. His TV *(break)*. *(when)*
5. I *(admire)* the view. I *(trip)* and *(fall)*. *(when)*
6. It *(snow)*. We *(make)* a snowman. *(While)*
7. Marcia *(clear)* the table. I *(do)* the dishes. *(two actions are in progress at the same time)*

8 Practice

Have a competition! Go to page 90.

GRAMMAR FOCUS

The past continuous: information questions

Wh- word	was/were	subject	verb + -ing	when or while clause
When	were	you	dancing?	
What	were	you and Grace	doing	when your brother came in?
What	were	you	doing	while Bruce was sleeping?
Who	*was*		**verb + -ing**	
Who	was		dancing?	

9 Practice

Work with a partner. Pretend you are the police officer investigating the accident pictured on pages 66–67. Your partner witnessed the accident. In your notebook, write questions for your partner. Use the cues. Have your partner answer the questions.

1. What / do / when / accident / happen?
   You: *What were you doing when the accident happened?*
   Your partner: *I was watching the ducks cross the street.*

2. What / man in first car / try to do?
3. Why / woman / yell?
4. Who / drive / second car?
5. Where / you / sit / when / accident / happen?

10 Reading

Before you read, discuss this question as a class: What are the benefits of performing small acts of kindness?

Now read the article.

Teenager Transforms a Classmate's Life

One day, on Oprah Winfrey's TV show, the talk show host asked her audience to try to help others. When she made this challenge, a 17-year-old girl from Michigan was watching. The teenager decided to take Oprah's challenge seriously.

Soon afterwards, while she was sitting in the school cafeteria with her friends, she noticed a boy that she had seen before. He always ate alone and he never seemed to have any friends. Without saying a word to her friends, she went over and sat down next to him.

At first, the boy did not look at her. He continued to eat quietly with his eyes on his plate. When he finally looked at her, she smiled warmly. The boy was uncomfortable because he thought she was making fun of him. But soon he realized that she was trying to make friends with him. They started a conversation. While they were talking, the girl realized that he was the most interesting and intelligent boy she had ever met. She made sure she told him that.

Before this lunch, the boy used to walk shyly down the hall trying not to be noticed. Now he walks with his head held high. Before, he had few friends. Now, he sits with a group of friends at lunch. The 17-year-old girl has changed the way he looks at himself. When she accepted him, she made him feel confident. She, in turn, has also been changed by her own simple act of kindness.

11 Comprehension

Discuss the questions below.

1. What challenge does the 17-year-old girl respond to?
2. How does she respond to this challenge?
3. Why do you think the boy didn't have many friends?
4. Why is the boy more confident now?
5. How do you think the girl was changed by her act of kindness?

12 Speaking

Think about someone you know (or read about someone), who performed a simple act of kindness that changed someone else's life. Share your story with the rest of the class.

13 Your Turn

Work with a small group. Discuss how you can help others—even in small ways—at school, at home, or wherever you go.

Example:

Wherever I go, I can give people I meet a warm smile.

14 Writing

In your notebook, write the results of your discussion from Exercise 13. Then use the results to create a poster of the different ways people can help others. Decorate your poster. Post it on your class or school bulletin board.

Progress Check *Units 9 and 10*

Grammar

A. In your notebook, write sentences using the cues below. (3 points each)

1. China / big population in the world *(superlative)*
   China has the biggest population in the world.
2. Rome / beautiful / Paris *(as . . . as)*
3. This movie / bad movie / I have ever seen *(superlative)*
4. Superman the Escape / scary / The Steel Eel *(not as . . . as)*
5. Brazil / big / Mexico *(comparative)*
6. The book / good / the movie *(comparative)*
7. That test / easy / so far *(superlative)*
8. My neighbor / boring person / I know *(superlative)*
9. Julia Roberts / famous / Uma Thurman *(comparative)*
10. *Crouching Tiger, Hidden Dragon* / fascinating movie of all time *(superlative)*

B. Fill in the blanks with the simple past or the past continuous form of the verbs in parentheses. (2 points each)

Last Saturday, my mother *(1. take)* ___took___ my brother and me on a trip to a state fair in New York. My father *(2. work)* _____ that Saturday, so he *(3. not go)* _____ with us. We *(4. get up)* _____ at 5:00 A.M. on Saturday morning. We *(5. have)* _____ breakfast at 6:30 A.M. when I *(6. fall off)* _____ my chair. I had fallen asleep with the spoon in my mouth! It *(7. rain)* _____ when we *(8. leave)* _____. My mother *(9. not feel)* _____ well that morning because she was tired. Anyway, we *(10. drive)* _____ on a small country road when suddenly we *(11. see)* _____ around 20 cows in the middle of the road. They *(12. stand)* _____ there, taking their time. My mother *(13. honk)* _____

several times, but they did not move. They *(14. stand)* _____ in the middle of the road for more than an hour. Anyway, we *(15. not get)* _____ to the fair until after lunch.

C. In your notebook, write information questions about the paragraph in Exercise B. Use the past continuous and the cues below. (3 points each)

1. Who / work that weekend?
   Who was working that weekend?
2. Who / have breakfast at 6:30 A.M.?
3. Why / not feel well?
4. What / stand in the middle of the road?
5. Where / drive?

Vocabulary

D. Choose a pair of adjectives from the box to describe each item below. One pair is used two times. (1 point each).

fast—slow	high—low
long—short	heavy—light

1. Speed of a track athlete: *fast—slow*
2. Duration of a trip: _____
3. Length of a ruler: _____
4. Weight of a box of chocolate: _____
5. Height of a building: _____

Communication

E. Work with a partner. Write a dialogue comparing three songs or books. Use the example below as a model. (3 points)

A: Do you like the song "I Need to Know"?
B: Yes, but I like "Crash and Burn" better.
A: Actually, I like "Hanging by a Moment" the best of the three.

Wide Angle on the world

1 Reading

A. Read the article on sitcoms. Underline any difficult words and look for clues to their meaning. If you still don't know the meaning, look them up in a dictionary.

B. Circle the correct answer to complete each sentence.

1. People laugh when _____.
   a. they are surprised
   b. a sitcom is on TV often
   c. something is supposed to happen

2. Creating humor by having fun with words is _____.
   a. a translation
   b. an idiom
   c. wordplay

3. Humor is sometimes difficult to share with people who speak other languages because _____.
   a. all humor is wordplay
   b. some words and idioms are hard to translate
   c. humor is not universal

2 Speaking

Work with a small group. Talk about sitcoms.
Do you enjoy them? Why or why not?

3 Writing

Work with a partner. Think of a joke in your native language. Try to write the joke in English. Is it easy or difficult?

_____
_____
_____
_____
_____
_____

What's So Funny?

Everybody likes a good laugh. It doesn't matter where you're from. And the things that make us laugh are also universal, more or less.

Laughter happens, according to experts, because we're surprised. Something that isn't supposed to happen does happen. This normal human response is why American sitcoms like *Seinfeld*, *Friends*, and *The Simpsons* are popular around the world. They're filled with clever surprises.

For example, when Phoebe sings out of tune on *Friends*, we're surprised. Surely, she's got to know how badly she sings. But she doesn't, and that's the joke. Surprise also makes us smile when Kramer slides in the door on *Seinfeld*. That's not the way most people enter a room. These jokes are understood by everyone from Colombia to China.

Some kinds of jokes are more difficult to share. For example, much of American humor depends upon wordplay. In *Seinfeld*, George plays with the word *toast*:

"Toasting makes me uncomfortable.

But toast I love. Never start the day without a good piece of toast. In fact, let's toast to toast."

The surprise is that the word *toast* has two different meanings, but it's pronounced the same for both meanings. There shouldn't be words with two meanings! How do we know what George is talking about, *toast* (crisp, browned bread) or *toast* (to propose a drink in honor of someone)? Translating this joke can be a headache in most languages. Sometimes the joke is lost. But other times, a translator can find a way to save it.

Sumonmarn Vovoranart translates *The Simpsons* into Thai. She translates wordplay by looking for another way of saying the same thing. For example, a joke using the idiom "a piece of cake" doesn't mean anything in Thai. Instead, Sumonmarn translates it as "easy as peeling a banana." It has a similar meaning, and Thai people understand the joke.

Laughter is universal, even though it sometimes takes a translator to make a joke's meaning clear. Aren't you glad we can all share in the fun?

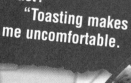

11 The talk show is taped there.

Learning Goals

Communication
Ask for and give additional information

Grammar
The passive voice: present tense

Vocabulary
Types of TV shows

1 Dialogue

🎧 **Listen and read.**

Stacy: Is this it? It's not much, is it?

Justin: I know. It's just stage lights and some cameras.

Guide: Well, right now, there isn't any taping going on. Do you see that set over there? A talk show is taped there every morning.

Steve: It's smaller than it looks on TV.

Guide: Yes, I know. By the way, the show is taped in front of a live audience.

Nicole: You mean, people like us can come and watch tapings?

Guide: Yes. Written requests are usually accepted once a year. Check the bulletin board on your way out. Schedules of tapings are posted there.

Stacy: Really? I didn't know that!

Justin: [whispering] Hey, Steve. Isn't that woman beautiful? I think she's going to appear on the talk show.

Steve: Justin, when it comes to spotting beautiful women, you're the best.

Justin: C'mon. I want to see her up close. Oops! Stacy! Are you all right? Oh, no, not again!

2 Comprehension

Discuss the following questions as a class.

1. Is Stacy impressed with the TV studio? How do you know?
2. What is Steve's impression of the TV studio?
3. How can people get to watch the tapings of some shows?
4. What do you think happened to Stacy? What makes you think so?

3 Useful Phrases

🎧 **Listen and repeat. Then match the phrases with the feelings they express. Write the letters.**

_c_ 1. Is this it? It's not much, is it?

_____ 2. I know.

_____ 3. You mean . . . ?

_____ 4. Really? I didn't know that!

a. It expresses agreement.

b. It expresses disbelief and surprise.

c. It expresses disappointment.

d. It asks for a clarification.

The passive voice: present tense

Affirmative statements

The show **is taped** there.

The episodes **are taped** in front of a live audience.

Negative statements

The show **is not taped** there.

The episodes **are not taped** by the director.

Remember! • Use the active voice to emphasize the subject as the performer of the action.

Martin **posts** the schedules every day.

• Use the passive voice to emphasize the subject as the receiver of the action. Form the passive voice by using a form of the verb *be* and a past participle.

The schedules **are posted** by Martin every day.

• Omit the *by* phrase in a passive sentence when the listener or reader does not need to know the performer of the action.

The schedules **are posted** every day.

4 Practice

Complete the sentences. Fill in the blanks with the passive form (present tense) of the verbs in parentheses.

1. I *(amaze)* _am amazed_ by the movie's visual effects.

2. He *(mesmerize)* _____ by her beautiful smile.

3. We *(awe)* _____ by our sister's intelligence.

4. Children *(fascinate)* _____ by fire trucks.

5. Tom Hanks *(respect)* _____ by his peers.

6. My little brothers _____ always *(reprimand)* _____ by our parents.

7. These days, most visual effects *(do)* _____ by computers.

8. Some cars *(run)* _____ by electricity.

9. In the United States, Spanish *(speak)* _____ by almost half the population.

10. These days, documents *(store)* _____ on computer hard drives.

5 Practice

The sentences below use the active voice. Rewrite them, using the passive voice.

1. Many writers hire literary agents.

   Literary agents are hired by many writers.

2. The writers write outlines.

   _____

3. Several writers study one script.

   _____

4. A main writer revises the first draft.

   _____

5. The director and the actors read the draft.

   _____

6. The writers make script changes.

   _____

7. The director and the actors approve the new script.

   _____

6 Vocabulary

Types of TV shows

A. 🎧 Listen and repeat.

1. News

2. Documentary

3. Talk Show

4. Situation Comedy

5. Home Decorating Show

6. Game Show

7. Cooking Show

8. Cartoon

9. Drama

B. In your notebook, copy the names of the different types of shows from Exercise A. Then write an example of each type of show. Use a TV guide for help, if necessary.

7 Information Gap

Student A, go to page 91. Student B, go to page 92. Follow the instructions.

8 Communication

Asking for and giving additional information

A. 🎧 Listen and read.

A: What's a sitcom?
B: It's short for "situation comedy."
A: But what does "situation comedy" mean?
B: It's a TV comedy series that focuses on a situation. It has a regular cast of characters and several episodes.

A: Can you give me an example?
B: Let me see. . . . I know. The TV show *Friends*—that's a sitcom.
A: Oh, I get it. Thanks!

B. Work with a partner. Write a similar conversation to Exercise A, using one of the types of TV shows in Exercise 6. Then role-play your conversation.

9 Reading

Before you read, discuss this question as a class: How do you think computers are used in film today? Then read the article.

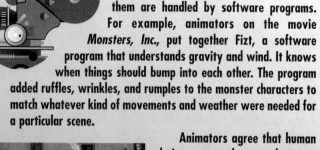

Movies and Computers!

The movie *Gladiator* takes place in ancient Rome. In one memorable scene, a gladiator is in the center of the great Coliseum, his opponent lying helplessly on the ground. The gladiator looks up at the emperor. Will the emperor give the thumbs-up sign and let the opponent live, or will it be thumbs-down, signaling death? When the emperor finally gives the thumbs-down sign, the crowd roars. The entire Coliseum is rocked by stomping and shouting. It is an amazing sight.

We are even more amazed by this scene when we learn that it is computer generated. Whenever a modern-day film has spectacular visual effects, chances are that animators and their computers produced them.

How is computer animation done? Animators use their knowledge of science to imitate reality on screen. Characters are created by human animators, but the details of their appearance and the environment around

them are handled by software programs. For example, animators on the movie *Monsters, Inc.*, put together Fizt, a software program that understands gravity and wind. It knows when things should bump into each other. The program added ruffles, wrinkles, and rumples to the monster characters to match whatever kind of movements and weather were needed for a particular scene.

Animators agree that human beings are the toughest to computer-generate because they are very complicated. Computers cannot understand the details of facial expressions and human emotions. "You and I can tell the difference between a fake smile and a real one, but try describing that to a computer," says Steve Maddock, a computer scientist. Perhaps that is good news for Tom Cruise—he won't lose his job to a computer!

10 Comprehension

Complete the sentences. Circle the letter next to the correct response.

1. The gladiator, the Coliseum, the emperor, and the spectators mentioned in the article are part of a _____.
   a. play   (b.) movie   c. song

2. Today, most of the amazing visual effects in movies are produced by _____.
   a. trained fighters   b. human actors
   c. computer animation

3. Fizt is _____.
   a. a computer program
   b. a human animator   c. a video game

4. Animators use their knowledge of _____ in computer animation.
   a. English   b. history   c. science

5. The most difficult subjects for animators to create are _____.
   a. humans   b. animals   c. machines

Learn to Learn

Learning English through movies and TV shows

Movies and TV shows use real-life English. From them, you can learn everyday words and expressions, correct intonation, and pronunciation. You can also learn about the culture of the country where the movie or TV show was made.

Back at the Hospital

🎧 **Listen and read. Why does Stacy want to be able to walk on Saturday?**

12 Learning English is cool!

Learning Goals

Communication
Talk about the value of extracurricular activities

Grammar
Reflexive pronouns
Gerund as subject, as object of verb, and as object of preposition

Vocabulary
Extracurricular activities

1 Dialogue

🎧 **Listen and read.**

Justin: This is great—another party! Ms. Costa, you are so cool!

Ms. Costa: Thanks. I enjoy giving parties, and it *is* the end of the semester soon.

Nicole: Everything looks good. Can we start eating?

Ms. Costa: Help yourselves.

Steve: Cool.

Ms. Costa: While you're eating, let's talk about a final project.

Justin: I knew there was a catch to this party!

Stacy: Stop complaining, Justin. What do you want us to do, Ms. Costa?

Ms. Costa: Well, . . . I'd like to encourage more students to join the Foreign Language Club. And I thought maybe you could develop a campaign for the club.

Nicole: That's a great idea.

Steve: Yeah, I don't mind helping. Count me in, Ms. Costa.

Stacy: Me too.

Justin: And Tom and me too. Joining this club has been one of the best things I've done this semester.

2 Comprehension

Discuss these questions as a class.

1. Why does Justin think Ms. Costa is cool?
2. What does Justin mean when he jokes, "I knew there was a catch"?
3. How does Ms. Costa plan to encourage students to join the Foreign Language Club?

GRAMMAR FOCUS

Reflexive pronouns

Subject		Reflexive pronoun	Example
I	⟶	myself	I hurt **myself** skating.
You	⟶	yourself	You shouldn't blame **yourself**.
He	⟶	himself	**He** laughed at **himself**.
She	⟶	herself	She cut **herself**.
It	⟶	itself	The wound healed **itself**.
We	⟶	ourselves	We watched **ourselves** in the video.
You	⟶	yourselves	You should help **yourselves** to sandwiches.
They	⟶	themselves	They enjoyed **themselves** at the party.

Remember! A reflexive pronoun is a pronoun that ends in *-self* (or *-selves*). It refers back to the subject of the sentence.

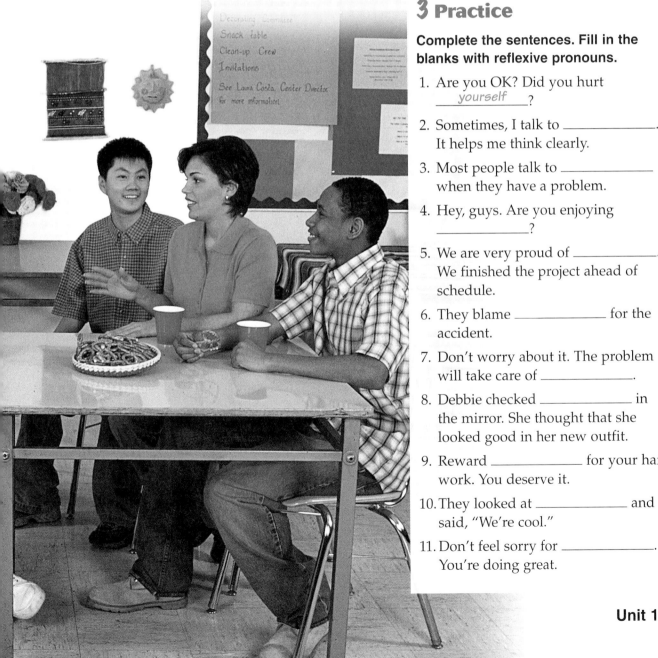

3 Practice

Complete the sentences. Fill in the blanks with reflexive pronouns.

1. Are you OK? Did you hurt
   ___*yourself*___?

2. Sometimes, I talk to _____.
   It helps me think clearly.

3. Most people talk to _____
   when they have a problem.

4. Hey, guys. Are you enjoying
   _____?

5. We are very proud of _____.
   We finished the project ahead of
   schedule.

6. They blame _____ for the
   accident.

7. Don't worry about it. The problem
   will take care of _____.

8. Debbie checked _____ in
   the mirror. She thought that she
   looked good in her new outfit.

9. Reward _____ for your hard
   work. You deserve it.

10. They looked at _____ and
    said, "We're cool."

11. Don't feel sorry for _____.
    You're doing great.

GRAMMAR FOCUS

Gerund as subject

subject	verb	
Learning a new language	is	cool.

Gerund as object of a verb

subject	verb	object of verb
I	enjoy	**learning** a new language.

Gerund as object of a preposition

subject	verb	preposition	object of preposition
He	is thinking	of	**learning** French.

These verbs can be followed by gerunds:

admit	imagine
avoid	keep on
begin	(continue)
can't help	like
consider	love
discuss	mind
enjoy	miss
explain	practice
feel like	prefer
finish	stop
hate	suggest

Remember! A gerund (the base form of a verb + *-ing*) is a verb that functions as a noun. A gerund can be used as the subject of a sentence, as the object of a verb, or as the object of a preposition.

4 Practice

Underline the gerunds. Then, write *S* if the gerund is used as the subject or *OV* if the gerund is used as the object of the verb.

1. __*S*__ Having friends is important in a teenager's life.

2. _____ Nicole likes spending time with her friends.

3. _____ I can't help calling friends for advice.

4. _____ Talking to parents can really help.

5. _____ Many people suggest discussing problems with parents.

6. _____ Keeping a journal is a great form of self-expression.

7. _____ Joining after-school activities can enrich a teen's school life.

8. _____ Avoid over-scheduling your activities.

9. _____ Spending time with your family is important, too.

10. _____ Parents miss having their children at the dinner table.

5 Practice

Below is the Foreign Language Club's poster inviting students to join the club.
Complete the sentences. Fill in the blanks with the gerund form of the verbs in parentheses.

The Foreign Language Club Wants You!

Hi, I'm Stacy Morgan. (1. Join) _____ the Foreign Language Club was the best thing I ever did for myself. In addition to (2. introduce) _____ me to new people, FLC has made school life more fun for me. Join us next year!

Hello from me, Justin Carlson. I never liked (3. join) _____ school clubs before. I thought they were boring. FLC has changed my mind. Now I love (4. go) _____ to FLC meetings. There is always something different going on at the club. Try it. You'll like it.

Hi. My name's Nicole Green. I used to be really shy, but (5. be) _____ a member of the Foreign Language Club has made me less shy and more confident. (6. Attend) _____ the weekly FLC meetings and (7. volunteer) _____ with young students have helped me deal with many kinds of people. Join the club. It can change your life.

I'm Tom Bryant. I've always loved (8. learn) _____ new languages. That was why I joined FLC. I'm glad I did. You should, too. Imagine (9. have) _____ fun, (10. meet) _____ wonderful new friends, and (11. practice) _____ a new language in a fun environment. Join us next year!

Hi, I'm Steve Liu. I enjoy (12. volunteer) _____ and (13. go) _____ on field trips. Thanks to Ms. Costa and the Foreign Language Club, I was able to do both this year. I will remember this year as my best year in school. Make your school life memorable. Sign up for the FLC next year.

6 Listening

🎧 The Foreign Language Club members are visiting classrooms to invite students to join FLC. Listen to the question-and-answer part of the presentation. Then write *T* for true, *F* for false, or *NI* for no information for each statement below.

__T__ 1. The FLC members are inviting other students to join the club.

_____ 2. Ms. Costa talked about the Foreign Language Club.

_____ 3. Participating in school clubs is fun and relaxing.

_____ 4. It's OK to join just any organization.

_____ 5. School clubs are only for popular students.

_____ 6. Participating in school clubs can help students develop self-confidence.

7 Vocabulary

Extracurricular activities

Read the postings on the bulletin board. Then write the name of the organization. Choose the words from the box.

science club	drama club	yearbook	computer club	school band	art club

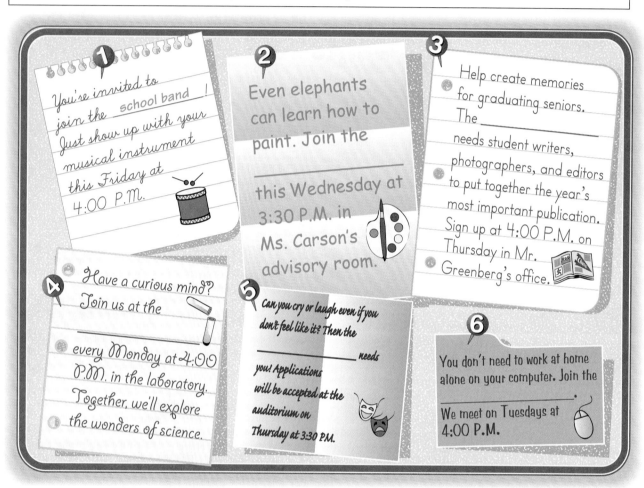

1. You're invited to join the **school band**! Just show up with your musical instrument this Friday at 4:00 P.M.

2. Even elephants can learn how to paint. Join the _____ this Wednesday at 3:30 P.M. in Ms. Carson's advisory room.

3. Help create memories for graduating seniors. The _____ needs student writers, photographers, and editors to put together the year's most important publication. Sign up at 4:00 P.M. on Thursday in Mr. Greenberg's office.

4. Have a curious mind? Join us at the _____ every Monday at 4:00 P.M. in the laboratory. Together, we'll explore the wonders of science.

5. Can you cry or laugh even if you don't feel like it? Then the _____ needs you! Applications will be accepted at the auditorium on Thursday at 3:30 P.M.

6. You don't need to work at home alone on your computer. Join the _____ We meet on Tuesdays at 4:00 P.M.

8 Your Turn

Work in small groups. Make a list of clubs offered in your school. Discuss what club or clubs you'd like to join next year and why.

9 Writing and Speaking

Work with the same group as in Exercise 8. Make a list of the benefits of participating in extracurricular activities. You may do research or interview other students to gather the information. Share your list with the rest of the class.

Participating in extracurricular activities can

help improve a student's self-confidence.

Learn to Learn

Developing your potential through after-school activities

Extracurricular activities can help you develop your potential as a student and as a person. Participating in school activities can lead to a higher sense of self-esteem, which can lead to a higher level of confidence and a better performance in school.

Progress Check *Units 11 and 12*

Grammar

A. Complete the sentences. Fill in the blanks with reflexive pronouns. (1 point each)

1. How was the party, Jenny? Did you enjoy *yourself* ?

2. He surprised _____ when he won.

3. Is that the new president? Let's introduce _____.

4. The students taught _____ to use the new software program.

5. She looked at _____ in the mirror and practiced her speech.

6. We keep promising _____ that we will exercise together.

B. Use the gerund form of the verbs in parentheses to complete the sentences. (1 point each)

1. I hate *(take)* *taking* our dog for a walk.

2. We considered *(invite)* _____ our relatives to the party, but we changed our minds.

3. *(Swim)* _____ is my least favorite activity.

4. My brother loves *(listen)* _____ to jazz.

5. *(Get up)* _____ early is difficult, especially on cold winter mornings.

6. *(Dance)* _____ is not one of my talents. I have no rhythm at all.

C. Look at the chart and the key. Then complete the sentences using gerunds. (2 points each)

	Wendy	Liza	Emil	Keith
1. read	✗	+	✔	✗
2. dance	✔	✔	✗	+
3. jog	+	✔	+	✗

Key	+ = *love* ✔ = *like* ✗ = *hate*

1. *(read)* Wendy and Keith *hate reading* .

2. *(read)* Liza _____.

3. *(read)* Emil _____.

4. *(dance)* Wendy and Liza _____.

5. *(dance)* Emil _____.

6. *(dance)* Keith _____.

7. *(jog)* Wendy and Emil _____.

8. *(jog)* Liza _____.

9. *(jog)* Keith _____.

Vocabulary

D. Write the types of TV shows under the correct categories below. (2 points each)

news	game show	cooking show
sitcom	documentary	home decorating show

Shows that inform	Shows that teach	Shows that entertain
1. _____	3. _____	5. _____
2. _____	4. _____	6. _____

Communication

E. Work with a partner. Complete the conversation below. (5 points)

A: Hey, _____?

B: A documentary is a factual and objective film presentation of a serious topic.

A: _____?

B: Hmm. A good example is that show on the building of the pyramids in Egypt shown on the Discovery channel.

A: Oh, I get it. _____!

B: You're welcome.

SONG

Savage Garden

In Brisbane, Australia in 1994, Daniel Jones advertised for a singer. He met Darren Hayes, and the two hit it off right away. They formed the group Savage Garden and began writing and recording songs together. By the time they broke up in 2001, they had become one of Australia's most successful bands.

CRASH AND BURN

When you feel all alone
And the world has turned its back on you
Give me a moment please to tame your wild, wild heart
I know you feel like the walls are closing in on you
It's hard to find relief and people can be so cold
When darkness is upon your door
And you feel like you can't take anymore

Chorus

Let me be the one you call
If you jump I'll break your fall
Lift you up and fly away with you into the night
If you need to fall apart
I can mend a broken heart
If you need to crash then crash and burn
You're not alone

When you feel all alone
And a loyal friend is hard to find
You're caught in a one-way street
With the monsters in your head
When hopes and dreams are far away
And you feel like you can't face the day

Repeat chorus

Because there has always been heartache and pain
And when it's over you'll breathe again
You'll breathe again

When you feel all alone
And the world has turned its back on you
Give me a moment please
To tame your wild, wild heart

Repeat chorus four times

1. 🎧 Read the lyrics. Find words that rhyme with the words below. Then listen to the song and check your answers.

   | floor   mall   say |

2. Circle five words or phrases that show someone feels sad and alone.

3. A friend is feeling depressed because his or her relationship ended recently. You want to comfort your friend. Write a short letter to him or her, using *If you . . ., I'll . . .*

GAME *True or False?*

Steps

1. Play this game in groups of three.

2. Each person flips a coin; the person with the most "heads" in three throws goes first.

3. Player 1 chooses one of the cues below and makes a statement that is either true or false.

4. The other two players ask two questions each about the statement. Then they guess whether the statement is true or false.

5. The player who guesses correctly gets a point. If both players guess correctly, they both get points and flip to see who goes next. If no one guesses correctly, the speaker gets a point and makes another statement.

6. The player with the most points at the end of the game wins.

The most exciting place I ever visited was Paris, France.

Yeah, right!

What did you do when you were in Paris?

The most exciting place I ever visited was _____ .

I hurt my _____ while I was _____ .

When I was a child, I was fascinated by _____ .

Last year, I was really proud of myself because I _____ .

The scariest experience of my life was when I _____ .

I'm thinking about _____ next year.

Fun with Grammar

Unit 2, 6 Practice, page 12

For the teacher:

1. You will need a very soft ball for this game. Arrange students in a circle, either standing or sitting at their desks.
2. On the board, write enough irregular verbs in their base form for the class, or divide the class into two groups. Have each group play the game separately.

> **Suggested verbs:**
>
> | | | | |
> |---|---|---|---|
> | 1. begin | 6. cut | 11. get | 16. sing |
> | 2. build | 7. do | 12. hurt | 17. speak |
> | 3. buy | 8. eat | 13. know | 18. take |
> | 4. choose | 9. feel | 14. leave | 19. wear |
> | 5. come | 10. find | 15. read | 20. win |

3. Start the game by calling out the first verb on the list. Then toss the ball to a student. That student should give the simple past form of the verb and toss the ball to the next student. The second student should say the second verb on the list and toss the ball to the next student, who should give the simple past form of that verb.
4. This game is meant to be quick and snappy. A student who is unable to give the correct form tosses the ball on to the next student and is disqualified from the game.

Unit 5, 11 Practice, page 35

For the teacher:

1. Before you play this game, you might want to review the names of the parts of the body.
2. Have students stand up. Tell them that they will be playing "Simon Says."
3. Stand up or have a leader you have chosen stand up and give commands and polite requests.
4. The students follow only the polite requests. For example:

Leader: Put your hands on your stomach.
Class: [*They do not follow the command.*]
Leader: Please touch your head with your right hand.
Class: [*They touch their head with their right hand.*]

5. If a student follows a *command*, that student is disqualified and sits down. The last student to remain standing wins the game.

Unit 6, 4 Practice, page 40

For the teacher:

1. Write list A below on a sheet of paper; write list B on another sheet of paper.

List A		List B	
1. slow	7. clear	1. late	7. quiet
2. beautiful	8. heavy	2. easy	8. good
3. good	9. easy	3. clear	9. safe
4. safe	10. early	4. early	10. hard
5. hard	11. late	5. slow	11. heavy
6. fast	12. quiet	6. fast	12. beautiful

2. Divide the class into two teams. Give list A to Team A and list B to Team B.
3. Have each team write the adverb for each adjective in the list. Give the teams 40 seconds to complete the exercise.
4. After 40 seconds, tell the students to put down their pens or pencils.
5. Have a representative from each team go to the board and write the adjectives and the corresponding adverbs on the board. The team who gets all the items correct wins.

Unit 7, 7 Practice, page 48

For the teacher:

1. Write the base forms and the past participle forms of the verbs below on the board and have students copy them onto a piece of paper. Give the class five minutes to memorize the base forms and their past participle forms. After five minutes, erase the lists.

Base form	Past participle form	Base form	Past participle form
1. be	been	11. keep	kept
2. bring	brought	12. know	known
3. choose	chosen	13. leave	left
4. do	done	14. lose	lost
5. eat	eaten	15. put	put
6. feel	felt	16. read	read
7. find	found	17. stand	stood
8. get	got, gotten	18. take	taken
9. go	gone	19. wear	worn
10. hit	hit	20. write	written

2. Write the base forms on the board, this time in a different order. Tell the class to write the past participle forms as fast as they can. Give them two minutes to finish the task. After two minutes, have students exchange papers and correct the answers. The student who gets the most correct answers wins.

Fun with Grammar

Unit 9, 6 Practice, page 62

For the teacher:

1. Write the following adjectives on the board:

1. high	6. small	11. new	16. safe
2. funny	7. soft	12. fat	17. lazy
3. good	8. bad	13. difficult	18. far
4. thin	9. pretty	14. wonderful	19. young
5. intelligent	10. smart	15. noisy	20. sad

2. Have students make three columns in their notebooks and head them **Positive**, **Comparative**, and **Superlative**. Then have students copy the adjectives from the board in the first column. In the second column, have them write the comparative form of the adjectives. In the third column, have them write the superlative form of the adjectives.
3. Give students five minutes to complete the activity.
4. The student who gets the most correct answers wins.

Unit 10, 8 Practice, page 69

For the teacher:

1. This is a memory test. Divide the class into two teams. Then refer them back to the picture on pages 66–67.
2. First, have the class agree on a name for each person in the picture. Then tell them to study the picture carefully. Give them one minute.
3. Next, tell the class to close their books.
4. Have each team choose a secretary, who will write down all the sentences that the team dictates.
5. Have each team create as many sentences as they can about the picture. The sentences can use either the simple past or the past continuous, or both the simple past and the past continuous. Give the teams three to five minutes to complete the activity.
6. Have the secretary from each team go to the board and write the team's sentences.
7. Each team gets a point for a sentence that uses either the simple past or the past continuous correctly, or both correctly. The team with the most points wins.

Information Gaps

Unit 5, 8 Information Gap, page 34

Look at the ad. Complete the information in your ad by asking Student B questions.
Student B should use complete sentences in his or her responses.

A: When will the dance party be?
B: It'll be on Saturday, February 14.

DON'T MISS
THE COOLEST DANCE PARTY OF THE YEAR!

at the George Washington High School Gymnasium
on _____ from 7:00 P.M. to _____.
Come dance to the beat of hip-hop, rock,
and world music! Live bands!

Lots of food, including _____ and _____ from Mario's!

Unit 11, 7 Information Gap, page 77

Look at your TV guide. Ask Student B for the missing information.

A: What's on channel 2 at 7:30 tonight?
B: Let me check the TV guide. Seven-thirty, channel 2, *Hollywood Squares*.
A: What type of show is it?
B: It's a game show.
A: I don't really like game shows. What's on . . . ?

Channel	7:00	7:30	8:00	9:00
2	Entertainment Tonight (Hollywood and celebrity news)		48 Hours Investigates (news magazine)	CSI (police/detective drama)
5		Simpsons (cartoon)		Seinfeld (sitcom)
21	BBC News (news)		Hometime (home decorating show)	

Information Gaps

STUDENT B

Unit 5, 8 Information Gap, page 34

Look at the ad. Complete the information in your ad by asking Student A questions. Student A should use complete sentences in his or her responses.

B: Where will the dance party be?
A: It'll be at the George Washington High School Gymnasium.

**DON'T MISS
THE COOLEST DANCE PARTY OF THE YEAR!**

at the _____
on Saturday, February 14 from _____ to midnight.
Come dance to the beat of _____, _____,
and _____! Live bands!

Lots of food, including pizza and soda from Mario's!

STUDENT B

Unit 11, 7 Information Gap, page 77

Look at your TV guide. Ask Student A for the missing information.

B: What's on channel 2 at 9:00 tonight?
A: I'm not sure. I think it's *CSI*. Let me check. Yes, It's *CSI*.
B: What type of show is it?
A: It's a drama—a detective drama.
B: Cool. What's on . . . ?

Channel	7:00	7:30	8:00	9:00
2	Entertainment Tonight (Hollywood and celebrity news)	Hollywood Squares (game show)	48 Hours Investigates (news magazine)	
5	Newscast (news)		That '70s Show (sitcom)	
21	BBC News (news)	Best Chefs (cooking show)		Ireland (documentary)

Project 1   A Snapshot of a Historical Place

Write about a historical place you visited in your town or city or on a trip, using the simple past and the simple present tenses. Use the project below as a guide.

A. Write where the historical place is and why it's famous.

Mount Vernon is just outside Alexandria, Virginia. Mount Vernon was the home of George Washington, the first president of the United States. George Washington lived there most of his life. During that time, Mount Vernon was a big farm, and George grew vegetables, raised animals, and made most of the things he needed there.

B. Describe the place.

George Washington's house is now a museum. It is a large, white, wooden house with a red roof. There is a large porch in the back. The house is surrounded by farmland and smaller buildings. There is a kitchen building (for cooking food), a wash house (for washing laundry), a smokehouse (for smoking meat), a spinning room (for making clothes), and even a shoemaker's shop. But none of these buildings are still in use today.

C. Write what you can do there today.

If you visit Mount Vernon today, you can tour all the rooms in the main house with a tour guide. You can also go out on the back porch and enjoy a great view of the Potomac River. You can visit the different buildings on the farm and even pet the farm animals. There is also a great hiking trail if you like nature. And there are lots of gift shops if you want to shop for souvenirs.

D. Write about the place's location, hours, and admission fees. Also, tell about the length of the tour.

Mount Vernon is about a ten-minute drive from Alexandria, Virginia, or a twenty-minute drive from Washington, D.C. It is open seven days a week throughout the year. Admission is $9.00. The tour lasts about three hours, but you can spend all day at Mount Vernon, if you have the time.

Project 2 Snapshots of Interesting Experiences

Read the projects below. Then write about three interesting experiences you've had, using the projects below as a guide. Share your project with your partner, group, or class.

Choose three topics from the list to the right, or choose your own three topics. Illustrate your project with personal photos or pictures from magazines.

An unusual animal, reptile, or insect you saw
A famous person you saw or met
A famous place, city, or country you visited
A festival or parade you attended
A movie, play, or concert you saw
A sports game, tournament, or race you watched
An unusual food or drink you tried

I once saw a rattlesnake. In fact, it almost bit me. I was camping with some friends in the woods near my house last summer. We were cooking dinner over a fire when I decided to move a big rock to sit on closer to the fire. As I picked up the rock, I heard a rattling sound. Since it was dark, I bent down to take a closer look. There was a huge rattlesnake looking right at me and shaking its tail in the air. I jumped back, yelled, and ran away as fast as I could. When I went back with my friends to where the rattlesnake had been, it was gone. Of course, I didn't sleep very well that night.

A Rattlesnake

Disney World

Last summer, I went to visit relatives in Orlando, Florida. That was the first time I got to go to Disney World. It was really cool. I went on a lot of rides. Alien Encounter, the Haunted Mansion, and Space Mountain were my favorites. I also visited Epcot. I went shopping in a Japanese department store and ate at a Canadian restaurant there. At night, I saw the Electrical Parade. It was really amazing. I bought a few souvenirs—a Mickey Mouse hat, a glass Donald Duck figure, and a book about Disney World. I also had my picture taken with Mickey Mouse. It was a great experience. I'd like to go back again.

David Bowie

One Saturday, I read in a newspaper that David Bowie was rehearsing at a local college auditorium. I walked over to the auditorium and saw a big black limousine parked outside. I heard music coming from the auditorium. The side door was open, so I went inside. I couldn't believe it—there was David Bowie on stage with his band! The auditorium was empty except for his crew. I was very nervous, but I sat down in the back anyway and watched. Soon, a manager came over and asked me to leave, so I went outside and waited. About an hour later, Bowie came out. He was very friendly, and he gave me his autograph. Then he got in his big black limousine, and it drove away.

Project 3 A Snapshot of an Interesting Person

Write about the life of a family member, friend, or famous person. Find out about that person's life by interviewing him or her or by researching his or her life. Then write a biography, using the project below as a guide. Share your project with your partner, group, or class.

A. Write about the person's birth, childhood, and youth.

Antonio Banderas was born on August 10, 1960, in Malaga, Spain. His father worked for the government and his mother was a teacher. As a child he was very active and energetic. He liked playing sports and dreamed of being a professional soccer player. But at age 14 he broke his foot in an accident. This made it impossible for him to follow his dream. Instead, he began to study acting at the School of Dramatic Art in Malaga.

B. Write about events in the person's youth.

When he was 19, Antonio moved to Madrid and joined an acting group. He was performing in a play when he was noticed by the film director Pedro Almodóvar. Antonio was cast in several Spanish movies by Almodóvar, and he eventually caught the attention of the American film industry. When he appeared in his first American movie, *The Mambo Kings*, Antonio could hardly speak any English and had to learn his lines phonetically. After that, he studied English intensively.

C. Write about achievements in the person's adulthood.

Antonio Banderas went on to make a string of hit movies: *Philadelphia* with Tom Hanks, *The Mask of Zorro* with Catherine Zeta-Jones, and *Evita* with Madonna. He met the actress Melanie Griffith in 1995 while he was filming a movie with her. They married in May of 1996 and soon after had a daughter, Stella Del Carmin.

D. Write about what the person is doing now or will do in the near future.

Antonio continues to make hit movie after hit movie. He and his family split their lives between two houses—one in Los Angeles and the other in Spain. Raising his daughter to know and understand both Spain and the United States is very important to him, as is having her speak both Spanish and English. According to Antonio Banderas, he and his family have the best of both worlds.

Zoom in on Culture 1

Greetings

Thailand

In Thailand, people wai when they meet. They put their palms together with fingers pointing upward. Then they position their palms in a way that shows their relationship to the people they are greeting. For example, when greeting friends, people position their joined palms in front of their chests because the friends are equal. When greeting respected people—teachers, parents, or elders—they position their joined palms at their foreheads. And, when greeting a very respected person, people kneel on the ground, bow, and wai with their joined palms at their foreheads.

Japan

In Japan, people bow when they meet. As with the wai, the way people bow shows the relationship and the situation. For example, in formal situations, when greeting a respected person, people bend almost 45 degrees at the waist with their eyes looking downward at the floor. The longer they hold this position and the more times they bow, the greater the respect. In semi-formal situations, when meeting someone for the first time, people bow at the waist at about a 15-degree angle. And in casual situations, when greeting friends, people just do a quick lowering of the head or head and shoulders and look at each other.

from Around the World

France

In France, people often "air kiss" when they meet people they know. They lean forward, put their cheeks together, and make a kissing sound. Then they change cheeks and do it all over again. In Paris, people usually kiss four times, but in other parts of France, they usually kiss two or three times. Men only kiss other men if they are very, very close friends or family members. Women kiss both men and other women they know. When meeting someone of the opposite sex for the first time, though, both men and women usually just wave or shake hands.

New Zealand

The native Maori people in New Zealand do the hongi when they first meet someone. They put their left hand on the other person's shoulder and shake hands as they lean forward and touch their noses and foreheads together for a couple of seconds. This gesture means that their minds are together and that they are breathing the same air. In some parts of New Zealand, Maori touch noses once, and in other parts they touch noses twice.

1 Comprehension

A. In your notebook, answer the following questions.

1. How are the *wai* and the Japanese bow similar?
2. How do a man and a woman greet each other in France when they are meeting each other for the first time?
3. How do the native Maori people of New Zealand do the *hongi*?

B. Work with a partner. Practice the Thai *wai*, the Japanese bow, and the New Zealand *hongi*.

2 Discussion

Work in a small group. Answer these questions.

1. Which way of greeting seems the most unusual to you? Why? Which seems the most familiar?
2. How do you greet people in different situations? For example, how would you greet:
   - a classmate for the first time?
   - your school principal for the first time?
   - your grandparents?
   - a close friend?
   - a boyfriend or a girlfriend?

3 Writing

Work with a partner. Using the descriptions of greetings in other countries as a guide, write how people in your country greet each other in three different situations.

Dining around the World

In **American** restaurants, your waitperson will often tell you his or her name and make small talk[1] before taking your order. He or she will automatically bring you a glass of water and try to keep your glass full throughout the meal. Adults will sometimes order wine, but it is illegal for anyone under 21 to be served alcohol. When you want your waitperson to come to your table, you should make eye contact. It is considered rude to call out or wave your hand at your waitperson. In the United States, you can order whatever you like from the menu. If you are not hungry, it is acceptable to order just a salad. For a full meal, you order soup, then a salad, and then the main course. The main course usually comes with vegetables. After dinner, the waitperson will bring you a dessert menu or describe the day's desserts (usually sweets, such as cake, pie, or ice cream). You should leave a tip of 15 percent to 20 percent of the total bill. If you don't think the service was very good, you can leave less.

1. **make small talk**: chat; talk about unimportant topics

In a traditional **Japanese** restaurant, you will take your shoes off and leave them near the door. Your waitperson will quietly take you to your table, where you will sit on a cushion on the floor. It is considered rude if the waitperson is too talkative. Your waitperson may serve you hot tea, but if you want water, you will need to ask for it. When you want your waitperson to come to your table, you will need to raise your hand and call out loudly "Sumimasen!" ("Excuse me!"). In Japan, you usually order a lot of small dishes. A full traditional meal usually consists of soup; then small servings of vegetables, meat, fish, and seafood; and then rice. Dessert, if any, is usually fresh fruit, followed by hot green tea. In Japan, you will usually be given chopsticks, but most restaurants keep knives, forks, and spoons for foreigners. Tipping is not practiced in Japan. If you leave money on the table, your waitperson may run after you to return it.

In Italy, your waiter will first ask you what you want to drink. If you order water, it will be bottled and you will have to pay for it. Children often drink wine with their dinner. When you want your waitperson to come to your table, you can call out "Cameriere" for men and "Signorina" or "Signora" for women. You can also wave your hand. A full meal at a traditional Italian restaurant usually consists of bread, then an appetizer, then pasta, then the main meat course, and then salad or vegetables. Pasta is not considered a main course, so you should not order it as your main course. Dessert can be fresh fruit, an assortment of cheeses, or an assortment of sweets, including tiramisu[2] or gelato[3]. Dishes are served in a leisurely way, and a meal can last two to three hours. The restaurant will usually add a 15 percent service charge to your bill, but it is polite to leave an extra 5 to 10 percent for the waitperson.

2. **tiramisu:** a small cake dipped in a liquid, such as coffee, and filled with a rich cheese filling
3. **gelato:** an Italian sherbert made from whole milk, sugar, gelatin, and flavoring.

1 Comprehension

Decide which countries practice the restaurant customs listed below. Write *A* for America, *J* for Japan, and *I* for Italy. Some items have two responses.

1. Pasta is not considered a main course. _____

2. Water is not free. _____

3. Children drink wine. _____

4. Children cannot drink wine. _____

5. You take your shoes off and leave them near the door. _____

6. You should tip your waitperson. _____

7. Rice is served at the end of the full meal. _____

8. Salad is served at the end of the full meal. _____

9. A meal lasts between two and three hours. _____

10. Waitpersons are talkative. _____

11. For service, you should call or wave to the waitperson. _____

12. One kind of dessert is cheese. _____

2 Discussion

Work with a partner. Discuss your responses to the questions below.

1. Which do you prefer? Why?
   a. a talkative waitperson or a quiet waitperson?
   b. children having wine at dinner or children not having wine at dinner?
   c. calling to the waitperson or making eye contact?
   d. ordering many small dishes or a main dish?
   e. tipping or not tipping?

2. Which restaurant customs in America, Japan, and Italy are similar to restaurant customs in your country? Which customs are different?

3 Writing

Write about restaurant customs in your country. Use the articles above as a guide. Include these topics: calling for a waitperson, ordering water and drinks, ordering a typical restaurant meal, and tipping the waitperson.

Singapore

Singapore is a republic[1] in Southeast Asia, south of Malay. It includes Singapore Island and 50 other islands. Singapore City lies on the southeast coast of Singapore Island. The country is one of the smallest countries in the world; it is also one of the richest.

Singapore was founded as a busy trading and port city by the British, and many different groups have come to live in Singapore over the years. For that reason, Singapore has become one of the most diverse[2] and cosmopolitan[3] places in the world.

Singaporeans include Chinese, Malays, Indians, and Europeans. There are four official languages: Chinese, Malay, English, and Tamil. TV newscasters say good night in all four languages, and you can see Indian movies with Chinese subtitles, or English movies with Malay subtitles. Singapore has one of the most diverse religious mixes anywhere: there are Buddhists, Muslims, Hindus, and Christians. In the old part of Singapore, you can walk down Arab Street, go through Chinatown, or visit Little India. And Singapore has some of the best restaurants in the world.

The climate in Singapore is tropical, and there is a wide variety of plant and animal life. Visitors to Singapore can explore the largest bird park in Southeast Asia or visit one of the world's best orchid gardens—with over 60,000 orchids. There's also the Night Safari at the Singapore Zoo, one of the world's most exciting zoo adventures. There you can walk or ride through thick jungle to see exotic animals that come out only at night. You can visit Underwater World—the world's largest aquarium—or see Volcanoland, with the world's most active (fake) volcano. If you get tired of the tropics, you can always visit the Snow City—a large indoor park where you can ski and snowboard on artificial snow.

Singapore City is one of the safest and cleanest cities in the world because of its very strict littering laws. Some people say the laws make Singapore City a better, safer, and cleaner city, but others say it makes the city too strict and boring. A visitor to Singapore will have to admit that it is one of the most diverse cities, one of the most urban islands, and one of the wealthiest and most beautiful countries in the world. There's simply no other place like it.

1. **republic:** a nation in which the power lies in the hands of the people entitled to vote
2. **diverse:** varied
3. **cosmopolitan:** representative of many parts of the world

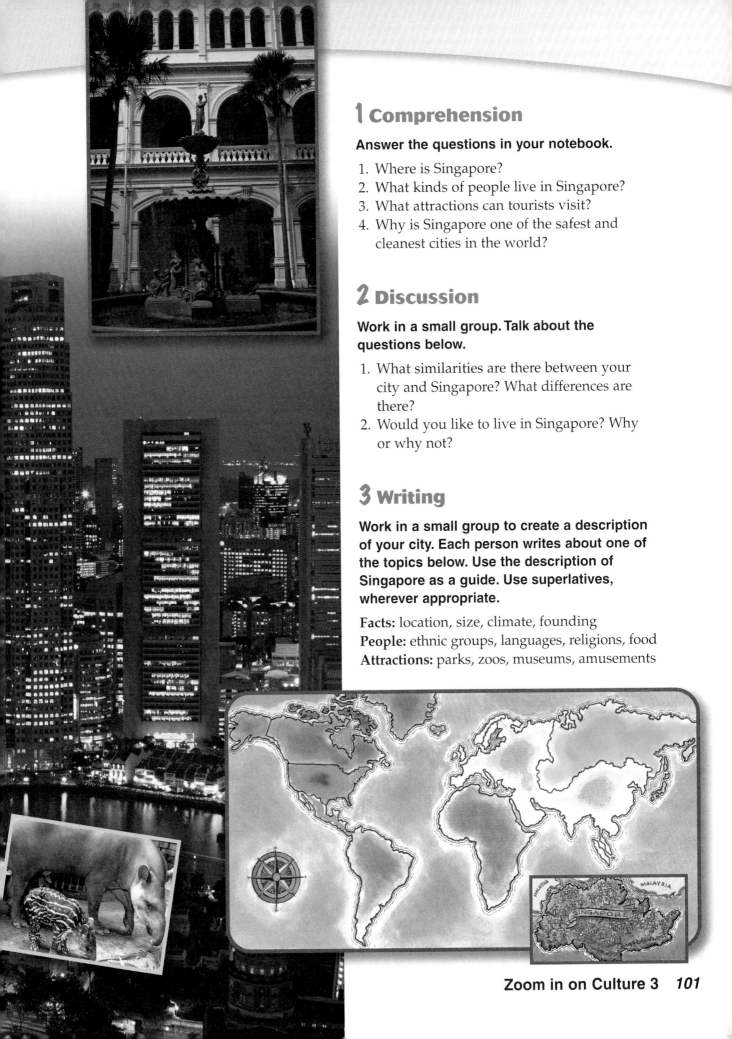

1 Comprehension

Answer the questions in your notebook.

1. Where is Singapore?
2. What kinds of people live in Singapore?
3. What attractions can tourists visit?
4. Why is Singapore one of the safest and cleanest cities in the world?

2 Discussion

Work in a small group. Talk about the questions below.

1. What similarities are there between your city and Singapore? What differences are there?
2. Would you like to live in Singapore? Why or why not?

3 Writing

Work in a small group to create a description of your city. Each person writes about one of the topics below. Use the description of Singapore as a guide. Use superlatives, wherever appropriate.

Facts: location, size, climate, founding
People: ethnic groups, languages, religions, food
Attractions: parks, zoos, museums, amusements

Useful Words and Expressions

UNIT 1

Nouns
adviser
after-school activity
backwoods
charity concert
conductor
ensemble
musical instrument
senior
surroundings

Adjectives
radical   agonizing

Verb phrases
head out
chat on the Internet
hang out with friends
get to know each other
go to parties
play the viola/cello/violin
raise money
run the show

Adverbs of frequency
always   sometimes
usually   rarely
often   never

Expressions
Welcome to (the Foreign
   Language Club).
My name's (Thomas). You can call
   me (Tom).
I'm (Stephen Liu). (Steve) for short.
See what I mean?
(Ms. Costa) is cool.
I'm just kidding.

UNIT 2

Nouns
conference   skyline
cypress tree   souvenir shop
host   walkways
oak tree   wildlife exhibit
orchid garden   willow tree
settlement

Verbs
Regular verbs:

Base form	Simple past
arrive	arrived
cry	cried
hug	hugged
prefer	preferred
travel	traveled
try	tried

Irregular verbs:

Base form	Simple past
go	went
have	had
take	took

Verbal phrases
run like clockwork
take a break

Adjectives
amazing   gentle
authentic   lush
brave   pleasant
efficient

Expressions
Why don't we . . . ?
How about . . . ?
I had a great time.
Why don't we do something
   together?
Nah, I don't feel like going to (the
   theater).

UNIT 3

Nouns
household chores
nuisance

Adjectives
messy
stale

Verbs
have to/has to

Verb phrases
Household chores
do the grocery shopping
do the laundry
clean the (bed)room
clear the table
cook lunch (or dinner)
help with chores
iron the clothes
make the bed
vacuum the floor
wash the car
wash (or do) the dishes
water the plants

Expressions
I'm on call.
Somebody called in sick.
You won't believe this.
She goes off in a huff.
Why are you avoiding me?
Yes, I'm on my way.
That doesn't seem too difficult.

UNIT 4

Nouns
Sports
baseball   soccer
basketball   swimming
golf   tennis
running   volleyball
Sports locations
course   pool
court   track
field

Verbs + infinitive
agree   need
begin   offer
can't afford   plan
can't wait   promise
decide   refuse
fail   try
forget   want
hope   would like
learn   would prefer

Expressions
Count me out.
Consider me your hero.
Me neither.
No problem.
I don't enjoy sports.
She's not into sports.

UNIT 5

Nouns
Drinks
bottled water
milk
orange juice
soda
Entrees (main courses)
grilled chicken
New York steak
pasta special
seafood platter
Desserts
cheesecake
chocolate cake
ice cream
pudding
Salad
mixed green salad
Greek salad
Soups
chicken noodle soup
onion soup
tomato soup
vegetable soup

Verbs
Imperative
Stand up./Don't stand up.
Look out!
Please close the door./
　Please don't close the door.
Walk three blocks.
Don't turn right/left.
Go north/east on . . .
Make a left/right on . . .
Other verbs

hop	spin
kick	step up
rock	stomp
shake	turn
slide	

Expressions
Come on, you guys!
You're taking forever.
Are you ready to order?
Could you give us a few more
　minutes, please?
Sure. Take your time.
OK. What will it be?
Is that all?
What about me?

UNIT 6

Adjectives
amusing/unamusing
comfortable/uncomfortable
decisive/indecisive
exciting/unexciting
happy/unhappy
honest/dishonest
interesting/uninteresting
loyal/disloyal
patient/impatient
polite/impolite
practical/impractical
sincere/insincere

Adverbs

carefully	hard
comfortably	late
decisively	loudly
early	neatly
easily	quietly
fast	patiently
good	softly

Expressions
If there's any way I can help,
　you'll tell me, right?
I'm going to have to pass.
It's a deal.

UNIT 7

Nouns
**Clothes and personal
possessions**

belt	shorts
briefcase	skirt
coat	sneakers
dress	socks
earrings	slippers
jacket	sweater
jeans	top
necklace	vintage clothing
pants	wallet
purse	watch
shoes	

Verbs

Base form	Present perfect
attend	have attended
be	have been
buy	have bought
check	have checked
go	have gone
have	have had
know	have known
like	have liked
love	have loved
meet	have met
play	have played
see	have seen
shop	have shopped
try	have tried
want	have wanted
wear	have worn

Expressions
Check these out.
Straight out of the '60s.
It's not my thing.
I can relate to that.
Yeah, that's it.
Do you need any help?
We're just looking.
Do you have this in red?
Here you go.
Can I try it on?

UNIT 8

Nouns

appearance	lifestyle
attitude	trend

Adjectives

confident	outgoing
demanding	strict
influential	

Expressions
Bummer!
How come?
Too bad.
I hope I get (Ms. Barr) next year.
Who do you have for English?
That teacher gave him a *D*.
I did OK on the test.

Useful Words and Expressions

UNIT 9

Nouns
ride
roller coaster
speed
TV network

Adjectives
Measurement
high–low
short–long
heavy–light
fast–slow

Comparative and superlative form of regular adjectives

bigger than	the biggest
cleaner than	the cleanest
cooler than	the coolest
friendlier than	the friendliest
hotter than	the hottest
more important than	the most important
longer than	the longest
newer than	the newest
more popular than	the most popular
more powerful than	the most powerful
scarier than	the scariest
slower than	the slowest

Comparative and superlative form of irregular adjectives

worse than	the worst
farther than	the farthest
better than	the best

Expressions
Well, duh!
Let's save the best for last.
By the way, . . .
Absolutely!
That was the most fun I've had in a long time!
Guess what?
In your dreams.
Seriously . . .

UNIT 10

Nouns
accident   hospital
challenge

Action verbs in the simple past form

bounced	cut
broke	fainted
burned	fell
crashed	kicked
crossed	sprained

Expressions
Watch out!
Are you all right?
I don't think so.
Should I call 911?
I'm really sorry.
It was my fault.
I wasn't paying attention.
Let's get the two of you to a hospital—just to make sure you're OK.

UNIT 11

Nouns
Entertainment
cast of characters
director
draft
episode
literary agent
live (audience)
outline
script
show
taping

Types of TV shows
cartoon
cooking show
drama
documentary
game show
home decorating show
news
situation comedy (sitcom)
talk show

Verbal phrases
approve the script
make script changes
revise the first draft
write outlines

Expressions
Is this it? It's not much, is it?
I know.
You mean, . . . ?
Really? I didn't know that.
Oh, I get it!
Can you give me an example?
Let me see . . .

UNIT 12

Nouns
Extracurricular activities
art club
campaign project
computer club
drama club
school band
school newsletter
science club
sports club
student council
yearbook

Reflexive pronouns

myself	ourselves
yourself	yourselves
himself	themselves
herself	

Verbs followed by gerund

admit	hate
avoid	imagine
begin	keep on (continue)
can't help	mind
consider	miss
discuss	practice
enjoy	prefer
explain	stop
feel like	suggest
finish	

Expressions
Help yourselves.
I knew there was a catch.
That's a really wonderful idea.
Count me in!
Join us!